Hanging On:
A Painful Pilgrimage

One Woman's Journey Through Grief

Deborah Young

M&B Global Solutions Inc.

Hanging On: A Painful Pilgrimage

ISBN 10: 1-942731-18-3
ISBN 13: 978-1-942731-18-4

Published by M&B Global Solutions Inc.
Green Bay, Wisconsin (USA)

Dedication

To those who have lost a loved one.

May it help you on your own journey.

"For I know the plans I have for you," says the Lord.
"They are plans for good."
Jeremiah 29:11 (The Living Bible)

Contents

Deborah Young

Acknowledgements

So many people helped me along this journey—Jeane Smits at Proko-Wall Funeral Home and Crematory, who aided and supported me from the onset; my aunts, Estell Childs and Mildred McDaniel, who never stopped believing in me; other widows who took the time to listen to me when they had endured their own painful journeys; my family at Our Saviour Lutheran Church in Green Bay, Wisconsin, especially those in Bible study who helped me see hope in the midst of despair; friends who showed me how to enjoy life again; and most of all God, who did not abandon me, but walked beside me every step of the way.

Special thanks to David Hatch, the pastor at Our Saviour Lutheran Church; Marie Haskins, who helped me at a time when she had her own burdens to bear; Edith Barth who always reminded me how blessed I was to have loved; the strong women in my class who kept my spirit and hope strong; and my co-workers at Prevea Therapy Institute, especially Maureen Mommaerts, who taught me how to smile again.

Also, particular thanks go to Mike Dauplaise, Bonnie Groessl and Amy Mrotek at my publisher, M&B Global Solutions Inc., who helped bring this book to life.

Prologue

As a young girl growing up on a farm in the flatlands of Illinois, I had a dream to one day write a book. This is not that book. Never had I envisioned embarking on the journey I share with you and never had I truly realized the pain that consumes one after the death of a spouse.

As early as junior high school, my writing teachers said I had a real knack for bringing my experiences to life in my prose. I had been searching for a way to heal when God reminded me of those instructors. By allowing others to join me, my story could not only help me, but others to heal and understand this complicated passage we call grief.

Early on in my grief process, I sought out books to discover if I had done things correctly. Preparation for a funeral had never been part of my repertoire, and though Jeane Smits from Proko-Wall Funeral Home & Crematory proved to be a wonderful guide, some things had been left entirely up to me. Nowhere could I find a book on grief that covered dealing with those initial details.

I also sought out confirmation that I had not lost my mind. I heard voices—Willie's, God's—and I answered them. Out loud. I did not hear the stage cues of a director, though, so my emotions went up and down. Solace came in clinging to the inanimate, things Willie touched or wore or he left his scent upon. Surely, my children would have me committed if they'd known.

I have written this book in chronological order, but it need not be read from cover to cover. I wanted the chapters to stand alone so even a little snippet could be helpful. I wanted them to be brief, as I know the limited attention span of a grieving person. I wanted to help those who grieve and those who want to understand the grievers.

Secondly, I wished to bring some awareness to chronic pain sufferers. So many hear, "I want my pain pills." What they don't hear is, "I want to feel good today." People who have chronic pain endure their own grief.

Grief differs for each of us as it is dependent on several factors. This is my journey and how I coped. If you are grieving, I encourage you to find things you can relate to and discover things that helped—or can help— you along the way.

Find supportive people for your story. And if you wish to help someone who is grieving, be one of those people.

Part One

Departure

I Miss You Most

I miss you most . . .
In the morning when I wake
When it's tea, not coffee, that I make
When the newspaper I no longer take

I miss you most . . .
In the day when I hear our song
When it's my dance partner for whom I long
When everything seems to go all wrong

I miss you most . . .
In the night, when in the bed I've rolled
When I wake and my feetsies are cold
When I only have your pillow to hold

I miss you most . . .
In the quiet of our home when I am alone
When talking to family, to friends on the phone
When I'm in places we're known or unknown

I miss you most . . .
In the week if the rain drops dare to fall
When storm clouds are dark and the wind calls
When the sun is bright or snowflakes fall

I miss you most . . .
On the days when work is what's ahead
When I have somewhere else to be instead
When my day is free and I can lie in bed

I miss you most.

Chapter 1

An Ordinary Day

October 18, 2012, was a morning like any other.

I woke up before Willie and wrapped my arm around him. After giving him a gentle kiss on the back of his shoulder, I slipped out of bed and headed to the kitchen to put the coffee on. He looked peaceful there, lying on his side of the bed with the brown and tan damask print quilt pulled up to his waist, his upper body bare. Part of me wanted to stay and snuggle with him, but it was a weekday and I had to go to work.

I reveled in the quiet morning and the lone sound of the coffee brewing. As I sat at the kitchen table, I closed my eyes before taking in a breath deep enough to inhale the smell of fresh coffee. What a great way to start the day. Usually about this time, I'd hear Willie get up and head into the bathroom. Not this morning. I thought he must be really tired today.

Quickly rejecting the idea of letting my sweetie sleep in, I went to wake him up when the coffee was done. But he did not even stir when I called to him. I reached out and shook his leg. "Come on, darling. Let's go. Don't make me late for work."

No response. I flipped the light on, since that always elicited a groan and he'd pull the covers over his head. But this time he didn't budge.

I moved up to his shoulders and gave him a little nudge. Then a little bigger nudge. Then more. Still no response. Nothing. I began calling out his name. Louder. Louder. LOUDER! My heart raced, my cheeks were wet, my vision blurry. I shook Willie until both his body and the bed vibrated as though they were in the midst of an earthquake. Still nothing.

I began swearing at him. "Darn it, darling! You have to get up!" Nothing. I began to panic. I ran upstairs and woke up our son, Bud.

"Help me! You have to help me wake up your dad. He won't get up. Bud, please help me get your dad up!"

No matter how hard Bud shook Willie's shoulder or how loudly he called out, "Dad!" he couldn't wake up Willie either. We dialed 911.

"I can't wake up my husband. Please help me!" The woman on the phone asked me to turn Willie over. He was heavy. Bud had to help me. The right side of Willie's face was squished. His right eye was just a slit. My heart sank. The woman started talking me through CPR. I screamed at her. "I know how to do CPR!"

I shoved the phone at Bud. He fumbled it in his hands and his large, brown eyes appeared blank behind his black-rimmed glasses. "Just answer her questions, Bud." I said firmly.

After checking for respirations and a pulse, I gave Willie two rescue breaths. His lips were cool. I cursed myself. We don't do rescue breaths first anymore! Even as I climbed across the top of him, I could not get the feel of those cold lips out of my mind. I began chest compressions. Had I looked for my landmarks? I didn't even know. *C'mon. You can do this. You work in health care. You positively affect lives every day. You can do this.* I put more force behind the compressions. I could hear the snap of the xiphoid. Oh, how my heart ached at that sound and still from my sweetie, nothing. Nothing at all.

Police arrived. Emergency medical techs. Our pastor. Our daughter. Someone put an arm around me and guided me out of the bedroom, past the collage of family pictures hanging in the hallway, through the kitchen where the smell of coffee still lingered, to the black leather sofa in the living room. These strangers in my home promised me they would do everything they could. Their faces held empathy. I could see they had spoken those words and offered this solace before. An emptiness surrounded me. I could not explain it. I felt robbed of sensation while I sat and waited for them to wake up my husband.

In the end, no one could wake up Willie. All efforts were futile. God took my sweetie home. Tears flowed and flowed. Although I cried out, nothing changed.

In disbelief, I went to Willie's side. He lay on his back atop the copper-colored sheets, dressed only in his black underwear. The covers had been tossed aside. Quickly I removed the electrodes stuck to his chest. He hated to have those awful things stuck to his skin. I tossed everything in the trash—the electrodes, the saline bag, and all its tubing. Then I pulled the blankets back up to his waist so he wouldn't get cold.

My daughter, Rachael, knocked gently at the bedroom door and spoke in soft tones. "Mom, is it all right if Pastor Dave comes in now?" She sounded strong and I was grateful for that. I had no idea where I would find my courage or my strength. Pastor Dave came in and prayed for us. My daughter and me and Willie. I had no idea where Bud was.

They left me alone then. Alone with Willie. I lay my head on his chest and the tears continued to flow. My hand rested on his sternum and I let my fingers run through his chest hair. I closed my eyes and strained to hear his breath, to feel the rise and fall of his rib cage. In our one-sided conversation, I kept asking him to please answer me.

Propping myself up on my elbow, I looked closely at his face. The peace his face displayed contrasted the turmoil churning inside of me. I ran my hand over his silver curls while I reminded him how much I loved him. The tears I wiped from his cheek were my own, but the area didn't stay dry long. I snuggled against him again, in the crook of his arm so he could comfort me. Nothing is better than being held by your sweetie when you are down and out.

I don't know how much time passed before the medical examiner arrived. I did not leave my husband's side. The medical examiner, dressed in casual professional attire, entered the bedroom with a pen and clipboard in hand, but he didn't seem cold and indifferent. Rachael showed him in. She stayed, no doubt to help me through a difficult question-and-answer session. To his credit, he offered condolences prior to beginning what was a routine task for him. After establishing some basic demographic questions, he began asking about Willie's body systems. "Did he have any heart trouble?"

Rachael began to answer. "It's possible. He had . . ."

I interrupted my daughter midsentence. "Your father always had a good heart! Always! There was nothing wrong with your dad's heart! NOTHING."

"I know, Mom." She put up her hands as if in self-defense. "Dad always had a good heart. I am not saying that he didn't." She excused herself from the room, informing the medical examiner that she would be in the other room if he needed anything.

I talked to him about Willie's medical history. I joked about the CPAP machine, how Willie liked to sleep with it more than with me. He would tease me like that, but he always offered me his kissy lips before he put the mask on. I closed my eyes and I could picture him, mask in hand, smacking his lips, awaiting that all-important goodnight kiss before he placed the mask on his face. I wiped tears from my face.

The question-and-answer session continued while I sat on the bed next to my husband and the medical examiner knelt on the carpet next to the bed. There were more questions on Willie's health history, his medications, and general information. Then something I never contemplated, "Which funeral home do you want to use?"

My heart raced. Willie and I had talked only minimally about funeral plans and never about a funeral home. Perhaps Proko-Wall? I had no idea, but I had been to services there and they did a nice job. I called for Rachael and sent her off to check with Pastor Dave. He probably knew better than I did. Rachael returned. Yes, Proko-Wall.

The medical examiner offered his condolences a second time and he was gone. Alone with my husband, I lay my head upon his chest and talked to him between the tears. I cried. I cried. I cried. I did not want to let him go.

I heard more people in the house. The funeral home folks had arrived. Still I would not leave Willie's side. Once I moved, he would be gone. Never again could I lie upon his chest. Never again could I run my fingers through his hair. Never again could we lie side by side in our bed, in our room, in our home.

October 18, 2012, was a morning like no other.

The Lord is close to the brokenhearted and saves those who are crushed in spirit. Psalm 34:18

Chapter 2

The Best Laid Plans

Rachael called quietly to me from the bedroom doorway. "Mom? Some guy named Bob and another dude are here from the funeral home." Her voice was tender, but cautious, considering my fragile mental state. Did she fear I might go off the deep end? "There's no hurry, Mom. They just wanted you to know."

I didn't respond. I couldn't.

Bob, middle-aged and balding with a clean-shaven face, wore a button-down shirt and dress slacks. He stepped around Rachael and into the bedroom as I lifted my head off my husband's chest. He offered condolences and reached for my hand. "I'm sorry to meet you under these circumstances, Mrs. Young." His demeanor did not betray the kindness in his eyes. "Please take your time. As your daughter said, we are in no hurry. We'll wait as long as you need us to."

Wait they did.

In my heart, I knew eventually I would have to let Willie go. For now, I hesitated. Only God's strength could enable me to leave Willie's side, turning him over to strangers. Something surrounding these men let me know God was with them, so I had no qualms about how my husband would be treated. My uncertainties lie in being forever without him.

Reluctantly, I left the bedroom. Bob and his assistant went right to work, laboring quietly and efficiently. Secretly, I hoped to hear my sweetie object to all this treatment, perhaps shouting out, "What do you think you're doing?" as he flailed his arms and flung the body bag aside. However, muffled voices were all I heard. This bad dream apparently wasn't going to end.

When they had my husband ready for transport, Bob presented me with some papers. Even in death you can't escape the dreaded paper-work. We scheduled a time to meet at the funeral home. Rachael took the papers. She became my rock.

I couldn't watch as they departed with Willie in a black body bag. I'd seen body bags on television shows—*CSI*, *Criminal Minds*, and *NCIS*. I'd seen them in the nursing homes where I had worked. Never had I watched one meant to take half of me away.

A state of disbelief still enveloped me. This morning, I woke up a wife, but now plans had all changed. Demand after demand came at me, and I felt totally ill-equipped to handle them. What was happening? I was not ready for this. I needed time to grieve. Bowing my head, I prayed for this nightmare to end.

It was only the beginning.

Everything became a whirlwind. Time no longer waited for me. Decisions must be made and things gathered. Speaking with Pastor Dave, I had mentioned seeing my husband's baptismal certificate. Pastor Dave suggested using it as a unique cover for the bulletin. Now, where had I seen it? The newspaper wanted a photo. Which one should we use? The funeral home wanted military records. Where did we keep them? Why was I not more organized?

By this time, our granddaughters, Jasmine and Alexia, and our oldest daughter, Brenda, had arrived. More branches of our family tree, all present to assist me, to free me up to shed more and more tears.

A little at a time, Rachael attempted to fill out the paperwork from the funeral home. She skillfully seized opportunities when I felt I could answer whatever they deemed necessary to know about my husband. My husband. Could I still call him that?

Suddenly I felt the urge to retrieve Willie's wedding band from the safe. I remembered the day we went shopping for our rings. After several other stops, we walked hand in hand, practically skipping, into Machesney Park Mall. He smiled like a lovesick teenager, though we were young adults. That smile warmed my heart. We took our time selecting the simple gold bands, something signifying our love and our commitment to one another. We found the perfect rings at Rogers & Holland. What a special day for us!

Now, I rolled his ring between my fingers. I held it close to me. I cried . . . some more.

> *Again I looked and saw all the oppression that was taking place under the sun: I saw tears of the oppressed-and they have no comforter. And I declared that the dead, who had already died, are happier than the living, who are still alive. Ecclesiastes 4:1a,2*

Dressed to a Tee

"Mom?" Silence. "Mom." Rachael again, invading the trance that overtook me this morning. Turning my head toward her, I hoped my eyes would be answer enough.

"We are supposed to take clothes for Dad to the funeral home. Is there anything particular that you want?"

Shifting my weight in the kitchen chair a quarter turn, I sighed before struggling to stand and headed to the bedroom, my daughter not far behind. Once in the bedroom, I collapsed on the corner of the queen-size bed my husband and I had shared and stared at the whispering wheat-painted walls, searching for answers. Silently, I prayed. "God, I don't know how to do this."

And God gave me Rachael.

Rachael pulled out her dad's one and only suit. "Do you want him to wear this?"

He always felt so handsome in that suit. He purchased it at Men's Wearhouse to wear to a friend's wedding, and he had since worn it to other special events. Normally, Willie wore a uniform and welding leathers for work, or a T-shirt and pair of blue jeans when he had the day off. Dress shirts and slacks had been part of his wardrobe for years, but not a single suit. He hadn't even donned a suit the day we married, just a nice white sweater and black slacks, but that is a whole other story!

In fact, I had never seen him in a suit until that day at the men's clothing shop. My thoughts wandered back to that day we shopped. I recalled when he stepped out of the dressing room. He opened the door and stood there waiting, dressed in a dark gray herringbone tweed jacket and black slacks, and adjusting a striped tie at the collar of a cornflower blue shirt.

"Well, what do you think?" he inquired.

What did I think? I was one lucky woman to be married to that good-looking man. "It looks really nice, darling."

"Yes, Rachael. I'd like him to wear that suit," I said. The suit was ideal for his funeral service, his coronation, when he received his crown from his Lord and Savior.

Rachael held up a dress shirt, a beige striped tie wrapped around the hanger. "What about this shirt and tie?"

I let myself fall back onto my elbows where I let a sigh escape. The striped tie did not seem appropriate. I pursed my lips and brought my eyebrows toward one another over the bridge of my nose. He certainly needed a tie for this occasion.

"I love the cornflower blue shirt, but let's use the tie I got him to wear at his class reunion." I leaned forward from my perch on the bed, opened his top dresser drawer and pulled out the tie. I ran it through my hands, feeling the cool sleekness of it once again. Closing my eyes, I recalled the story of the tie.

It had been a few years earlier when Willie planned to attend his class reunion in Illinois, and he wanted to wear his suit with the striped tie. However, prior to the reunion, I shopped at Heid Music with my daughter and granddaughter. A tie demanded my attention as I browsed the racks of musical merchandise.. Gently, I ran it across the palm of my hand. It was a beautiful tie: black and silky, with music staffs of white and treble clefs and notes in an electric indigo shade of blue. Willie was an eclectic music lover. Consequently, that tie made the perfect choice for him. I enjoyed surprising him with the musical tie as we dressed in our room at the Clock Tower Inn before we headed to his reunion.

"You really like this tie?" Willie asked while he knotted it at his neck.

"Are you kidding me? I love that tie. You will be the best-dressed man at your reunion. Trust me." Standing on the balls of my feet, I kissed his cheek. I loved more than that tie.

His tie was the hit of the reunion. His female classmates had to run it through their hands while offering him their compliments. Quite the tie, I hadn't considered how much attention it would garner, and at that moment, I wasn't sure I liked it after all. But today, deciding what my husband should wear for his coronation service, I knew he should have all the attention. I placed the tie with his suit, ready to take them to the funeral home.

"I'm glad that's done," I said, lying back onto the bed.

"Mom, they said everything. Socks, underwear, shoes," Rachael said.

"His shoes are under the bed in a maroon-colored box, and everything else is in the top drawer of his dresser," I said as I curled up in a fetal position.

Rachael opened the drawer and pulled out a pair of black crew socks. Suddenly, a shocked look appeared on her face. "I didn't know my father had a pair of these." Clasped between two of her fingertips, she held up a pair of red underwear, a white band around the top broadcasting "Be My Valentine." Ah, that did make me smile. Some things you just don't want to know about your parents.

One summer, Willie and I traveled to Florida. While there, we spent some time walking on Daytona Beach. Just off the beach, a small cluster of shops beckoned tourists with their "Sale" signs. Never one to pass up a bargain, Willie led the way inside the first shop. Delighted to find a great deal on tie-dyed T-shirts, he selected one in brilliant yellows, blues, and pinks, reminiscent of the 1970s. That shirt became Willie's signature shirt. He wore it everywhere, and we all loved how he stood out among the crowds when we went to the flea markets, Bay Beach Amusement Park in Green Bay, or other busy areas.

One Sunday morning, I exited the garage as my husband and son came out the back door of the house. I always dress up for church, a behavior my paternal grandmother instilled in me. Although I cannot recall what I wore that day, I distinctly remember my husband wore his tie-dyed T-shirt.

"I thought we were going to church?" I stated quizzically.

"We are," he answered.

"Well, are you going to get dressed?" I asked, raising my eyebrows for emphasis.

"I am dressed," he said matter-of-factly.

"That's what you're going to wear to church?" My eyebrows rose higher.

"Grandma always said it didn't matter what you wore to church, as long as you went," our son chimed in.

"You're no help," I said and we went off to church. Not only did God see my sweetie in church that morning, but so did everyone else.

My husband did know how to make me smile. The tie-dyed T-shirt would also go to the funeral home to be worn under Willie's suit.

I also placed his favorite Green Bay Packers cap and reading glasses with his suit. Willie needed one last thing: his ChapStick. He did not go anywhere without a cherry-flavored lip balm in his pants pocket. In a heart-to-heart one night, Willie shared his history about this little red tube, revealing to me his love for Suzy Chaffee, who first introduced cherry ChapStick via a series of television commercials in the 1970s. I couldn't compete with that love affair. I added a fresh tube of cherry ChapStick to the pile. Willie wasn't going just anywhere.

> *But the Lord said to Samuel, "Do not consider his appearance or his height, for I have rejected him. The Lord does not look at the things man looks at. Man looks at the outward appearance, but the Lord looks at the heart." 1 Samuel 16:7*

Chapter 3

Sharing Sweet Stories

When Rachael opened the passenger door, I just sat there, staring straight ahead. Still numb from the preceding events, I hardly knew how I got to Proko-Wall Funeral Home. Nausea had settled in my stomach and a constant pressure established itself in my head and my heart. Silently, I said a prayer for strength.

"Mom?" One word spoken, but Rachael asked so much more. Tenderly, she reached for my arm as though guiding a frail woman. "C'mon, Mom. You can do this."

But I did not think I could.

Bob greeted me just inside the funeral home doors. I recognized him from being at the house this morning and felt comforted to see a familiar face. Then he did the unthinkable. "Mrs. Young, this is Jeane. She will be assisting you."

The spinning in my head accelerated. How many more strangers would I need to interact with today when I only yearned to have my sweetie back? Would this bad dream be over anytime soon?

A sudden weakness seized my legs and I reached out for the nearby arm of one of my daughters. A voice inside my head made impossible demands. *Take me home. Let me start the day over. Give me my husband back! We always make important decisions together! I just want my husband! Why didn't anyone understand that?*

Jeane, a professional-looking woman, wore a navy skirt and a matching suit jacket layered over a white blouse. She stood a bit taller than me, forcing me to look up to see her dark brown eyes. Her well-kept chestnut hair, hanging a few inches below her shoulders, had a hint of curl at the ends. Her facial features exhibited softness.

She greeted us sympathetically. Verbal exchanges took place between Jeane and my daughters, Rachael and Brenda, but I felt miles removed. "Let's go back to a room where we can talk," Jeane suggested.

Jeane led us to a small room and offered seats around a white kitchen-style table. "Can I get you something to drink? Coffee, tea, water?"

Coffee? I definitely did not want coffee. What had become of the cups of coffee I had prepared for Willie and me this morning? Did they still sit untouched on the oak headboard next to the *Green Bay Press-Gazette* and its undone crossword puzzle?

Most of us said yes to a bottle of water. Jeane left the room to fulfill our requests. I looked at the faces of my granddaughters, Jasmine and Alexia, and my daughters. Our son, Bud, couldn't bring himself to join us, and as much as I longed to have him with me, I respected his decision. Everyone grieves differently.

I held tight to my husband's wedding band. Rolling it between my fingers comforted me. I took in a deep breath and brought the ring to my lips. Securing the band in my palm, I folded my hands together in prayer and held them close to my heart. I shut my eyes and transported Willie back to me.

Jeane returned with the water. She hadn't yet taken a seat when I blurted out, "Willie has to have his wedding band." I held it close, held it to my lips, held it to my heart. Closing my eyes, I could see his smile.

Jeane soothingly placed her right hand over mine. "He will have his wedding band. We will make sure of that. For now, I just want you to hold on to it. I can see it brings you peace." She reached for the paperwork Rachael had returned to her. "I can see you loved him very much. How did the two of you meet?"

"Through a mutual friend," I said. "We became friends, hanging out together. That all changed the night he stopped by my house to get a light for his cigarette." I smiled even though tears trickled down my cheeks.

"When I opened my front door, I found him leaning into the door frame, an unlit cigarette in his right hand. It surprised me because we had been together less than a half-hour before. He stood there with a grin across his face and said, 'Got a light?' I must have looked puzzled because he continued. 'You know I can't drive home without a cigarette.' I rustled up some matches for him. My brother, Donnie, had been there, and when Willie left, he said, 'He likes you.' "

I laughed. "I told Donnie we were just friends and he said, 'Deb, the guy just drove twenty minutes out of his way to get a light for a cigarette.' Then I realized Willie didn't just come over for a light."

"Dad always said Mom was a little slow," Rachael said, and we all chuckled.

"He loved being a grandpa," Brenda said. "Remember when I had Lexi? He had barely gotten to the hospital before he was leaving. I was thinking, 'What the heck, Dad?' He just wanted to spoil her right away. He had gone over to Sears and bought her all those clothes."

"Gramps was always buying me things," Alexia said. "Mostly animal books, because he knew I wanted to be a vet."

"Grandpa always took me to get strawberry pie," Jasmine said. "And not because I wanted to be a baker."

"Strawberry pie?" Jeane questioned.

"She and Dad would always sneak off to Perkins for strawberry pie in the summertime," Rachael explained. "It was their favorite. They'd come back and sit at the kitchen table together, eating their pie, laughing and talking between bites."

"Dad was always getting us things, but did you notice he never used the things we got him?" Brenda asked.

"He was always saving it until the one he was using wore out," Rachael said. "Like his Packer wallet."

"We always thought we should just rewrap those gifts and give them to him for the next holiday," Brenda teased. "Dad wouldn't have even known."

"Your dad hated for you girls to spend your money on him." I paused. "He hated you slamming doors, too. Remember when he took your bedroom door off?"

"That was the last time I stomped up the stairs and slammed my door. I still tell Bud and Rachael, whatever you do, don't slam the door," Brenda said. We all laughed.

Jeane listened attentively, jotting notes on the paperwork in front of her, as we continued sharing stories. Stories about a husband, a father, a grandfather. Stories about the man who changed my life, who gave me hope, who slept with me each night, who woke with me each morning . . . until this morning.

> *Therefore, strengthen your feeble arms and weak knees.*
> *"Make level paths for your feet," so that the lame may*
> *not be disabled, but rather healed. Hebrews 12:12-13*

It's All in the Details

Jeane brought in two large, white binders containing matching prayer and thank you cards, and asked us to look through them. We opened them slowly, as if that might somehow delay time. Each page displayed several cards, and we pored over them. I searched for something that fit my sweetie, something that felt like him, something that told his story.

"What about this one?" the girls said simultaneously. Each binder lay opened to the same page. The card in question pictured an old red barn.

Willie had grown up on a dairy farm in Illinois and loved visiting his childhood home. When his parents moved into a condominium, they had hoped we would move into the farmhouse that had been built by his ancestors in 1875. But work for welders had not been available in that area at the time, so Willie's dream to move back there had not been fulfilled.

The words on the thank you cards offered no options, but a wide variety of suggestions presented for the prayer cards. There were pages of beautiful, heartfelt words to peruse. With so many words to choose from, uncertainty surged on how we would ever decide. Then God provided us guidance as we read:

"God's garden must be beautiful,
He always takes the best.
He knew you were suffering.
He knew you were in pain.
He knew that you would never,
Get well on earth again.
He saw the road was getting rough,
And the hills were hard to climb.
So he closed your weary eyelids, and
Whispered, 'Peace be thine.'
It broke our hearts to lose you,
But you didn't go alone
For part of us went with you
The day God called you home."
- Author Unknown

We reached a unanimous decision. These words fulfilled our desire for the ideal verse.

Willie had suffered for a long time. A service-related injury continued to plague his knees, and a fractured left wrist that initially was misdiagnosed caused him almost continual agony. The pain in these joints created so many obstacles to the things he wanted to do both for himself and with his family. Still, he worked hard to support and care for us. My fingertips ran over the verse. Tears stung my eyes as I read over the words again. Yes, they were perfect for my husband.

Jeane placed more books on the table, flower books to be specific. Flowers typically conveyed joy. My mind flashed back to a summer day. When Willie arrived home from work, he found me in the backyard, a pink bandanna covering my head and a paintbrush in my hand.

"Hey, Sweetie. How are you?" Willie asked while kissing me on the cheek. He flashed me that boyish grin I adored and pulled a dozen red roses out from behind his back.

"What are these for?" I questioned as I reached for them. My birthday, our anniversary, or a holiday were months away.

The boyish grin disappeared. Willie's shoulders dropped. "I thought you liked flowers. You always buy them for yourself at the farmers market."

Smiling, I leaned in and kissed his lips. "I do, darling, I do. I love them! I just thought I had forgotten something is all."

"Mom, what about these?" Rachael's voice brought me back to the present. Flowers needed to be picked out for Willie now.

Another difficult decision with all the available options. Willie's flowers needed to reflect his roles, husband, father and grandfather, and our love for him. Finally, I opted for flowers in patriotic colors, white and blue carnations and red roses. He would have an American flag on his casket so they would be fitting. Royal blue ribbons with golden letters attached to the sprays would list the relationships.

I rubbed my temples. So many decisions to make and Willie had left me just hours earlier. What else would they ask of me?

"All this is in writing," David said, "because the hand of the Lord was upon me, and he gave me understanding in all the details of the plan." 1 Chronicles 28:19

Lay Him Down

Jeane led us into the casket room. The walls were lined with tiered shelves angled at forty-five degrees to display an assortment of caskets. The small room wrestled with my claustrophobia. Or could it still be the numbness? More uncertainty. What I did know for sure: yet another decision had to be made.

The casket would only be a temporary resting place for Willie as he wanted to be cremated. The caskets started at four hundred dollars for the rental of a simple metal box, and the price went up from there. How high, I didn't know. Although cost had to be considered, I didn't want money to be the deciding factor. How, then, does one select a casket? As a very young woman, I had to choose a casket for my dad. His six-foot-tall frame and a carriage for greater than 300 pounds narrowed the options to gold or silver.

Willie, a tall man at six foot one, didn't weigh nearly what my dad had, allowing us more options. Knowing how many sacrifices Willie had made for me fueled my determination to have every detail reflect him. My daughters and I looked carefully at the caskets with their array of finishes and satin liners in a variety of colors.

An oak casket with brass hardware caught the attention of each one of us. The beautiful wood grain and the hardware's patina reminded us of the furniture Willie refinished and loved so much. In my mind, I could see the Perry Davis medicine box we used to store pills, the Encyclopedia Britannica box we used for a book shelf, and the Daisy cheese box that corralled office supplies. His love for things that possessed character or suggested historical significance was like a chronic disease for Willie, something he inherited from his antique-dealing parents. This casket had the appeal of an antique.

I scanned it from end to end before running my hand over the wood, an action my husband did when he refinished a piece of furniture. Touch always told him so much about the piece he worked on, and nothing cleared inspection until passing the touch test. The casket's smooth surface allowed my hand to glide easily over it. Closing my eyes, I relied strictly on my fingertips. They told me this was the one.

We opted for a satin liner in ivory to complete the ensemble. Thinking all the necessary choices had been made, I headed for the door. However, Jeane pointed out the selection of guest books available in the same area. Another decision to make? At the moment, I just didn't care. "Girls, can you just pick one? I need to sit down," I said.

I ran my hand across my forehead. Hopelessness filled me. No time to rest. I doubted I would ever be together again. Half of me was gone.

But man dies and is laid low; he breathes his last and is no more. Job 14:10

Together Forever

Willie had asked to be cremated, so the next step was choosing an urn. A wide selection in all shapes and sizes sat on glass shelves in the next room. Similar in size to the room the caskets occupied, this one felt bigger with the open shelves and spot lighting.

Jeane spoke as we entered the room. "Over here we have vases if you want something to set on a mantle or a book shelf," she said as she swept her left arm wide. "Or, if you are thinking more of a chest, there are several here." A sweep of the right arm. "Or perhaps something for the garden. This one is a birdbath, but it is available as a sundial." None of us responded as we silently browsed the different pieces.

"Mom, how about this one?" Brenda asked, pointing out a box in a red, white, and blue tie-dye print. "Doesn't it make you think of Dad?" I nodded my head and turned up the corners of my mouth in a little grin. Yes, it did. But I believed in my heart we should keep looking.

I wandered back to the garden urn Jeane had pointed out when we first entered this area. Approximately three feet tall with a copper green base, it resembled an architectural column and emanated an air of history, and the cast bronze sundial sported an antiqued finish.

"That one is a companion urn," Jeane said.

"A companion urn?" I asked.

"Yes. It is made for two people, so for instance a mother and a child. Or, in your case, a couple. If you're planning to be cremated as well, you can have his ashes placed in there now and when you die, your ashes can be placed in there with his," Jeane answered.

A companion urn. Willie and I would be together.

I want to be cremated and I want to be together. The words echoed in my mind.

A zealous collector of cast iron, Willie spent his free time hunting, cleaning, and polishing the pieces in his collection. He amassed waffle and wafer irons, cake molds, skillets, Dutch ovens and his true passion, muffin pans. By rote, he knew the manufacturing companies and their histories, and could easily identify what year a particular logo had been used. His eyes sparkled and his heart raced whenever he discovered a new piece. He'd converse with others about his collection, whether or not they shared his passion.

Iron occupied space on every floor of our home. He'd laugh when he told people, "The house used to be three stories tall, but it sank from the weight of all the iron." Yet, the search continued. Griswold manufactured a sundial in the 1930s. It was one piece of iron my husband had lusted after but never found. Though not cast iron or a Griswold, the urn's sundial boasted the fine detail Willie had sought in a quality collector piece.

As an avid gardener, my enthusiasm lay in playing in the dirt, planting flowers, growing vegetables, and decorating my gardens, often with treasures Willie dragged home. A garden had always been a part of my life. Many times as children, my siblings and I found ourselves

25

weeding a garden row when our interactions had been less than stellar. We learned the value of teamwork while we reflected on our behavior. Gardening continued to be a form of meditation and relaxation for me.

Just as my husband's cast iron collection consumed more and more spaces in our home, my garden expanded into more and more areas of our yard. Digging up another grassy area guaranteed him giving me a hard time, similar to the harassment he received from me regarding his cast iron obsession. The thought caused me to smile.

I want to be cremated and I want to be together. I repeated the words silently.

"I like this one," I said. "With the sundial, I really think it reflects who your dad was and we both can have our ashes interred in it."

The style of the urn went together like we did, and that brought me comfort.

> *Then the Lord God made a woman from the rib he had taken out of man, and he brought her to the man. The man said, "This is now bone of my bones and flesh of my flesh; she shall be called 'woman,' for she was taken out of man." For this reason a man will leave his father and mother and be united to his wife, and they will become one flesh. Genesis 2:22-24*

Finishing Touches

"Hello?" Jeane said into the phone. "Yes, Pastor Dave. Yes, she is still here." Some details of the service needed to be coordinated with the church.

"Would Monday afternoon work for the service, Debbi?" Jeane asked. "And, did you want the gun salute?"

"We can do that?" I asked, worried it would not be possible with our church in the middle of the city.

We determined that my husband could have the gun salute. Willie, a Vietnam veteran, served his country at a time when the general feeling across the country was to spit on our returning soldiers rather than salute them. He seldom talked about his time in the service except to say he remembered being told to change out of his uniform before he got off the plane. The memory always haunted Willie. He had only stepped up to do what his country asked, and his brother had sacrificed his life in that war. My husband, an admirable man, should be honored as he left this earthly place and went on to heaven. He deserved that.

With those details worked out, Jeane led us into the final room, another small space. The unoccupied center of the room made it appear larger so the claustrophobic feelings subsided somewhat. Or perhaps, the knowledge of knowing the decision-making was nearly done had accomplished that.

"Here are all the extra things you may want," Jeane said.

Extras. It sounded like a wonderful thing. A bonus. But here, right now, in this situation? I had my doubts.

We entered the room together, all my girls and me. Inside we found crosses, flag cases, garden stones and other things. Embellishing a funeral service seemed strange, an oddity that I had never thought about. I longed to have Willie here to help me with all these decisions. Why did it feel like life was so unfair?

"Grandma, Grandpa should have a cross," Jasmine said.

"Do you want to help me pick one out?" I asked her. We selected a simple gold cross to hang on the lid of the open casket. Simple fit Willie and me. The cross, a reminder of the Savior who died for us, the promise of a better place, and a reminder of the peace my husband now experienced. *Thank you, Lord Jesus.*

The cross represented my husband's role in God's army. But he also served in the United States Army, so a flag would adorn his casket. We would need a case and opted for one in oak, a hard wood that Willie thought possessed a lot of character. I closed my eyes and envisioned the flag in the case, but not on the casket.

"Mom, one of these stones would be nice for the garden. You could place it next to the garden urn," Rachael said. "Here, what about this one?" She pointed to a flat, gray cement stone, engraved with words that expressed our feelings exactly.

> *"No farewell words were spoken,*
> *No time to say good-bye,*
> *You were gone before we knew it,*
> *And only God knows why."*
> *-Author Unknown*

God knew why, and though that provided some reassurance, my heart continued to ache. I closed my eyes. *Don't abandon me now, Lord. Yes, the Lord Giveth and the Lord Taketh Away.*

With our selections in tow, we headed back to the room with the white kitchen-style table. Jeane greeted us at the room's door, taking the items from the kids as they entered. "Alright. Now, we just need to schedule a time for the visitation here and for the service at the church," Jeane said.

"No. No. Everything will be at the church." I emphatically shook my head. Willie, a strong believer that everything that happened to us happened for a reason, knew God had a master plan for all of us. His sendoff needed to be in God's house, in the church. It was part of the plan. Everything should be done in one day at the church, starting with the visitation and culminating in the coronation service.

"We can do that. Let's plan for a three-hour visitation starting at one o'clock, with the service to commence at four," Jeane suggested.

"No, no. A two-hour visitation is plenty long enough," I said, unwilling to budge. Talking to people for three hours seemed a daunting task, one I felt unable to handle. I did not know if I could handle getting through life until Monday. *Why had we not died together?*

> *The Lord brings death and makes alive; he brings down*
> *to the grave and raises up. 1 Samuel 2:6*

Chapter 4

Music for the One I Love

Silence accompanied us on the short ride home from Proko-Wall, and I breathed easier knowing all the decisions had been made. Time to hide somewhere where the world would go away.

Rachael pulled the butane blue minivan into the driveway and turned off the ignition.

"You okay, Mom?" she asked.

"I'm doing okay," I lied.

"Good. We still have to select the hymns for Dad's service," she said.

Doesn't anyone understand I am grieving here? Why do I need to decide all this stuff?

"Yes, I know," I said, using every bit of energy I had to speak and maneuver myself out of the passenger side of the van.

Willie, a diverse music lover, listened to a wide variety of music ranging from easy listening to hard rock. When he sat and relaxed, he listened to music. When he worked in the garage, he played music. When he drove, one his many CDs would blare from the stereo. My favorite times were when he turned the volume up on the 1970s hi-fi in the basement, beckoning me to come and dance with him. When we dated, Elton John's "Sad Songs" would be the last dance of the evening. That would be the song blasting from the stereo.

He enjoyed picking out songs for us. Reaching for the volume button, he'd say, "Listen to this darling."

After listening to the song, he asked, "Don't you think that sounds like us?" One such song was "No Doubt About It," sung by Neal McCoy, a song about how things (or people) went together. I smiled as I remembered these little romantic tidbits. Now, it was my turn to pick out songs for him.

"I am sure you'll want 'Amazing Grace,' " Rachael said.

"Without question," I answered. Throughout our lives together, God had shown us amazing grace. Here now, when Willie's mortal life had ceased, he possessed a life of joy and peace because of that grace.

"I want to have 'The Old Rugged Cross,' too," I said. The hymn evoked many memories for me. The cross where Jesus suffered, shedding his blood to assure that one day we could share in his glory, was so important, especially now that my husband shared that glory.

One more hymn needed to be chosen. "What about the hymn we played at Grandma and Grandpa's funerals, 'Just a Closer Walk With Thee?' " Brenda suggested.

"That is a good hymn, but I was thinking about 'Softly and Tenderly Jesus is Calling,' " I said.

Both hymns were appropriate. The lyrics to "Just a Closer Walk With Thee" (Guide me gently, safely o'er, to Thy kingdom shore, to Thy shore) was exactly what we wanted for Willie, but so was "Ye who are weary come home" from "Softly and Tenderly Jesus is Calling." Willie was so weary.

"Can one of you email Pastor Dave and see if we can have four hymns? He said to choose three, but I don't know how we can do that." Pastor Dave gave the okay to select four hymns. *Thank you, God.*

Brenda and Alexia left then, leaving Rachael to be my sounding board. Lucky her. She stood behind me, brushing my hair gently in an attempt to comfort me as I spoke. I often played things over and over in my head when faced with making tough decisions. Brenda had offered to request friends sing at the service and I told her no.

"I can't believe your sister is pressuring me to have John and Jennifer sing at your dad's service. I already have so many things on my mind. Doesn't she realize that?" As I am verbalizing this, I come to realize how beautiful Willie's ceremony would be if the hymns were sung by people we knew.

"Hand me the phone!" I demanded and quickly dialed. "Brenda, can you call John and Jennifer and see if they will sing at your dad's service?" I asked. "I'm not thinking too clearly today."

In moments, Brenda returned my call. "Yes, they will do it. We just need to get them the hymns we want. Jennifer said she'd play the piano, too."

Beautiful voices to sing praises as my husband left us and joined his Lord and Savior. *Glory be to God.*

> *Speak to one another with psalms, hymns and spiritual songs. Sing and make music in your heart to the Lord, always giving thanks to God the Father for everything, in the name of our Lord Jesus Christ. Ephesians 5:19-20*

Words of Comfort

The late hour left me alone and sitting at my kitchen table, where I hoped to awaken from this nightmare. My heart grew increasingly heavy as reality set in. Time to tackle the next task: select the Scripture readings for the service. Holding my face in my hands, I found both of them wet with tears. I wiped them away and ran my hand over the Bible that sat before me.

"Oh God. Please guide me as I choose the words from your book.

Show me the words that not only will send my husband peacefully into your arms, but that will also provide comfort for those he leaves behind. Amen."

As I opened my Bible, I noted certain passages had been marked by words of inspiration from cards, clippings, and hand-written notes I had tucked inside. I perused those words first, but somehow, none of them felt right.

I rose and headed into our home office to get another translation of the Bible, my laden steps indicative of my troubled heart. When I returned to the kitchen chair, the burden I carried felt much heavier than the Bible in my hands. Choosing passages seemed an overwhelming task. I prayed for more guidance.

This Bible translation, The Living Bible, looked more like a college textbook with its highlighted passages and hand-written notes in the margins. Dog-eared page corners, tattered edges, and a well-worn cover indicated it as my go-to source when I sought God's leadership.

"Oh God, I know the words I seek are here, but I need your guidance to find them." Again I ran my hand over the Bible, then hugged it to my chest. More tears fell. I closed my eyes. When I felt I had the strength to go on, I set the Bible down on the table and opened it up, not to the pages marked with cards and clippings, but to the beginning as though about to read a great novel.

My intention was to scan the table of contents as I knew I sought three passages— an Old Testament, an Epistle, and a New Testament. As a child, I could name all of the books of the Bible by rote, but now some slipped from my mind without a visual reminder. Would that happen with my husband, too? Someday would he be a memory that required visual cuing? Oh, how my heart continued to hurt.

After I opened the cover and turned the title page, I saw a penciled notation I had made some years earlier: "1 Corinthians 29:15 Life." I turned to it then.

*"For we are here for but a moment, strangers, in the
land as our fathers were before us; our days on earth
are like a shadow, gone so soon, without a trace." TLB*

So much about death in a passage I noted for life.

Still feeling lost, I went back to the beginning of The Living Bible
for some direction. The initial pages included some commentary with
suggestions on reading the Bible; a chart to track your own reading,
where I was surprised to see I had read most of the Old Testament
when I was a mere nineteen years old; an article on how the Bible fit
together; and then, just what I was looking for. The page headed "How
this book speaks directly to you" gave me exactly what I wanted it to do
at that very moment. Slowly, I read through the phrases and found one
that said, "When you think about death." Paging through the Bible, I
went to 2 Corinthians where the words spoke to me, relating the exact
words that would bring me comfort at this time.

*For we know that when this tent we live in now is taken
down - when we die and leave these bodies - we will
have wonderful new bodies in heaven, homes that
will be ours forevermore, made for us by God himself,
and not by human hands. How weary we grow of our
present bodies. That is why we look forward eagerly to
the day when we shall have heavenly bodies which we
shall put on like new clothes. For we shall not be merely
spirits without bodies. These earthly bodies make us
groan and sigh, but we wouldn't like to think of having
no bodies at all. We want to slip into our new bodies so
that these dying bodies will, as it were, be swallowed
up by everlasting life. This is what God has prepared
for us and, as a guarantee, he has given us his Holy
Spirit. 2 Corinthians 5:1-5 TLB*

Those words brought me great comfort as I knew my husband no longer suffered with his earthly body. Pain had consumed and changed him to the point he no longer could complete the tasks his mind longed to accomplish. Every morning, he started the day out by swearing, a routine even he was unaware of. I did not realize at the time how much I would actually miss hearing those curse words!

That fulfilled my desire to have a passage from one of the epistles. I chose the Old Testament passage easily, the twenty-third Psalm.

> *The Lord is my shepherd, I shall lack nothing. He makes me lie down in green pastures, he leads me beside quiet waters, he restores my soul. He guides me in paths of righteousness for his name's sake. Even though I walk through the shadow of death, I will fear no evil, for you are with me; your rod and your staff, they comfort me. You prepare a table before me in the presence of my enemies. You anoint my head with oil; my cup overflows. Surely goodness and love will follow me all the days of my life, and I will dwell in the house of the Lord forever. Psalm 23*

Now I needed a passage from the Gospel. I began paging through the book of Matthew when a brief phrase drew my attention: *Rest for the Weary*, exactly what God provided for my husband. Though my heart ached, I knew Willie rested peacefully. I read on.

> *At that time Jesus said, "I praise you, Father, Lord of heaven and earth, because you have hidden these things from the wise and learned, and revealed them to little children. Yes, Father, for this was your good pleasure. All things have been committed to me by my Father. No one knows the Son except the Father, and no one*

knows the Father except the Son and those to whom the Son chooses to reveal him. Come to me, all you who are weary and burdened, and I will give you rest. Take my yoke upon you and learn from me, for I am gentle and humble in heart, and you will find rest for your souls. For my yoke is easy and my burden is light." Matthew 11:25-30

With the Gospel selected, I could now rest, even if only for a brief period of time.

As for God, his way is perfect; the word of the Lord is flawless. He is a shield for all who take refuge in him. 2 Samuel 22:31

Locks of Love

One more thing needed to be done for my husband. I preferred to wear my hair a little shorter, but Willie always liked it long. After Willie suffered a stroke three years prior, I re-evaluated that decision. Funny how choices are altered when the life of one you love is threatened. I decided the length of my hair didn't matter, so I kept it well below my shoulders just for him. He'd turn over in bed and roll right onto my hair. Though quite painful, the pulling of my hair when he caught it as he placed his arm around my shoulder proved to be even worse.

During these frequent times, I joked with him about my hair. "If you want my hair long, you know I'm going to send it with you if you go before I do."

Willie responded with a grin as he put his arms around me. "Go ahead, Sweetie. Put it right in the casket with me." He kissed the top of my head.

Although it wasn't an official promise, those words continued to

35

play in my mind. I knew I needed to give him my hair, needed to know he held it in his hand over his belly, the same place he could feel it when I lay on his chest when we snuggled in our bed together. Oh how I will miss those heart-to-hearts!

* * *

Friday. Willie passed away yesterday. Still feeling so sad and empty and not thinking clearly, I merely went through the motions with everything, including planning to get a haircut. My cousin Joanna agreed to take me to the salon. Thinking their mother was making a rash decision, my daughters remained a little apprehensive about it, but I would do anything for Willie.

Getting your hair done should be an exhilarating event. However, for me this day, the hair cut off would be of greater consequence than what remained.

Diane, the stylist, led me back to a black chair and sat me down in front of the mirror before covering me with a large apron. She ran her fingers through my blond hair. "What are you thinking today?"

"I need you to cut off my ponytail," I said. I heard my voice, flat, lacking its usual energy for life. The smell of hair dye and permanent solution assaulted my nose. I focused on taking shallow breaths in an attempt to dilute the odors.

"Oh. Are you going to donate it?" Diane asked.

"I need the ponytail." Again with the monotone voice. I struggled to keep my self-control. Tears could come at any time and I didn't want that to happen here in front of this stranger. I just wanted my hair cut.

"What are we going to do with the rest of it?" Diane questioned, still running her fingers through my hair.

"Do what you want. My husband is gone and I just need the ponytail to send with him." My voice raised an octave. All of these questions began to frustrate me.

I saw Joanna's look of concern. She put her magazine down and got up from the turquoise sofa.

Diane started combing out my hair, her smile replaced by a serious expression, sympathy. Joanna sat back down, relaxed again, but keeping her eyes on me.

"I'm sorry," I said. "I don't really know when I washed my hair last. I just don't remember."

Diane led me over to the sink and washed my hair, giving my scalp a good massage. My nose had acclimated to the scents, but my eyes had not yet become accustomed to the bright lights, so I closed them. I longed for the impossible—the touch of Willie's hand on my head, his arms around my shoulder tugging at my long locks, the liberty felt as he set my ponytail free.

Back in the chair, Diane brushed my hair back and banded it together. A swift clip of her red handled scissors detached my ponytail. She carefully placed it on the counter in front of the mirror. Women around me who were excitedly getting their own locks cut chattered and laughed. I remained quiet, staring straight ahead.

The woman in the chair next to me commented on my ponytail. "Wow. How long is that?"

Diane answered. "I didn't measure it." Her scissors snipped, hair flying in all directions, wet locks smacking the black plastic apron.

"That's a big change," the woman said. "You are going to have a hard time getting used to it."

Words did not come to me. Adjusting to short hair seemed miniscule compared to what I would have to get used to.

Though she was a friendly woman and meant no harm, I couldn't bring myself to interact with her. Diane did her best to answer for me without revealing my confidences. I thanked God for Diane.

Diane finished my hair and I paid her, adding a nice tip, before grabbing my ponytail and heading out the door. Joanna drove me to Proko-Wall. I requested they lay the ponytail across my husband's belly, just where he always liked it. My girls would have brought the ponytail to the funeral home, but they would never have provided the instruction that I wanted, that I needed.

My head felt as empty as my heart.

And now these three remain: faith, hope and love. But the greatest of these is love. 1 Corinthians 13:13

Chapter 5

Trip Down Memory Lane

" **A** re these all the boxes, Mom?" Rachael asked as she and Brenda balanced stacked cardboard containers while maneuvering down the stairs.

"We'll go back up and get that pile of albums, too," Brenda added.

Alexia, Jasmine, Bud, Joanna, and I each relieved them of some of their load before we all congregated in the living room. With the white chocolate walls, antique lamps, and large front window, it afforded us much light.

"I think that's all of them," I answered, still not really sure of anything.

The group of us, sprawled out on the plush, charcoal-gray rug, began sorting out photos, some many years old and others more recent. The funeral home provided boards for us to post pictures on and would also prepare a DVD. Together we laughed. Together we shared stories. Together we snickered at hairstyles and clothing.

At first, we merely sorted out the photos of Willie. Later, we could decide which ones would and wouldn't be included in the collages and the DVD. How amazing to see my living room carpeted in photographs. We had been blessed with many good times.

The whole process took longer than I had thought it would, but time became inconsequential. Reliving memories proved beneficial for all of us. Nothing helps one connect to a lost loved one like looking through old pictures. The healing process had begun.

Though we had several physical pictures, I still wanted to get some off the computer. Suddenly, it seemed sad that I no longer printed up photographs. No matter. If we wanted some, I would just order one-hour prints. That would be easy enough.

The photos on the computer basically encompassed the last five years. What wonderful trips we had had. What precious memories with our family. Some pictures stirred up some not-so-pleasant memories, too. Life, though not always a storybook, made us who we were.

Willie had dreamed of traveling across Lake Michigan on the SS Badger, a car ferry that traveled between Manitowoc, Wisconsin, and Ludington, Michigan. That dream, realized just two months before, flashed before me as I clicked through the electronic photo album. Walks on the beach elicited the feel of the breeze against my skin. The climb up the Empire Bluffs reminded me how Willie, in spite of his knee pain, had gladly climbed over a mile so I could have an eagle-eye view of Lake Michigan. Red, white, and blue petunias growing along the roadway brought forth images of the U-turns Willie had made so I could capture just the right angle. Another click of the mouse revealed Willie sitting at the stern of the ferry, waving good-bye. It had been taken when we headed home.

Then something struck me with the photos. As I related stories about people and places unfamiliar to the kids, I looked into my husband's eyes. I loved that twinkle he always had. He could say so much to me with those eyes. Now these photos on the computer showed me something I hadn't noticed. Or maybe I didn't want to notice. Over the last year, that twinkle had been replaced by pain. There was no mistaking the suffering in his eyes. My heart ached.

"Mom, are you doing okay?" Rachael asked.

"Just ordering some pictures," I responded. "Will you or Brenda go pick them up when they are ready?" Rachael nodded.

I set the computer aside and we laid out a carpet runner of photos for the DVD before narrowing it down to a throw rug. Still greater than the 100-picture limit, I weeded them down even more. Once we made the final selections, including those from the one-hour order, Rachael took them over to Jeane at the funeral home. When she returned, we worked on the collages, randomly placing pictures here and there until all four white foam boards had been completely covered.

My virtually non-existent appetite did not stop Rachael from getting up and putting food out for supper. Several friends had dropped off food and I contemplated what a blessing it is to have them in my life. Suddenly, I heard another knock on the door. I opened it, expecting a visitor bringing more food, but instead found Jeane standing on my wooden front porch, the finished DVD in hand.

"I knew you would be waiting for this," she said as she offered the DVD to me.

Jeane. Another blessing. Anticipating my needs even before I did.

When we finished eating, we watched the DVD of photos together. The photos on the big screen brought Willie to life for us and we reveled in the memories, in laughter and tears.

The final photograph flashed onto the screen. Willie sat at the stern of the car ferry, waving goodbye.

> *But Timothy has just now come to us from you and has brought good news about your faith and love. He has told us that you always have pleasant memories of us and that you long to see us, just as we also long to see you. 1 Thessalonians 3:6*

Something in Purple

Saturday morning, I sat in Willie's spot at the kitchen table. No coffee aroma infused the air. No one awaited a steaming cup of brew, an undone crossword puzzle, or a good-morning kiss. The sun, unaware, streamed its bright rays through the window pane, illuminating the oak sheen on the table. Had not the world ended?

I heard the squeak of the back door on its hinges just moments before Rachael appeared at the top of three steps that led from the back porch to the kitchen. The scrape of the front door against the frame announced Brenda's arrival at the front entry.

"Morning, Mom." Rachael spoke first. "What's the plan for today?"

I shook my head. "No plans." Lying became second nature. Had I not planned to wrap myself in Willie's bathrobe, inhaling his scent and feeling him close once again? To allow tears to flow freely, washing away this pain that shrouded my heart?

"I think we should go shopping," Brenda said.

Shopping? She had to be kidding. I hated shopping.

"You girls go. I'll be alright here. Your brother is home," I answered.

"Mom, you need a dress to wear for Dad's service," Rachael said. "So you need to come with." My apparel for the coronation service had not crossed my mind. My concern had only been on what Willie wore.

"I'll find something in my closet," I said.

"No, I think we need to go shopping," Brenda said, gently nudging me up from the chair. "Go get dressed and we'll wait for you."

Bless my girls who thought about their mother. However, something told me this trip encompassed more than just getting clothes. Shopping would become the diversionary tactic used to get me out of the house and focusing on something else.

I succumbed to their wishes and dressed in the same clothes I had worn the day before. A brush barely touched my hair and I failed to don any makeup.

"Let's go to JC Penney," I said and off we went. JC Penney carried the Worthington brand whose clothing I found fit me well, and had an easy wash and wear quality.

Feeling more like an automated robot than an excited shopper, I entered the department store with little enthusiasm. My thoughts veered toward something in purple. Willie liked me in purple, and even though this was supposed to be about me, I knew in my heart it was still about him.

Purple is a color that moves me spiritually. It transports me to Easter when our Savior rose from the dead. It takes me to spring when the lilacs bloom. In fact, many of the plants in my garden either have purple blossoms or purple leaves. Purple is a calming color. I needed that right now.

In the Misses department, I slid one hanger after another over on the rack, quickly vetoing each dress for one reason or another. Perhaps I found the neckline too round, too low-cut or so high it would set my claustrophobia into overdrive. Or maybe the sleeves were too long, too short, or over-embellished. The cut may have been wrong—too tent-like, too snug, not snug enough. The waist line or the hemline may have caused the rejection—too high, too low.

I found nothing just right.

Begrudgingly, I took two dresses to the dressing room, neither one purple. And as it turned out, neither a good fit. After hanging the garments on the rack outside the fitting room door, I found my daughters.

"Did you find something, Mom?" Rachael asked.

"No. They were all wrong," I answered. My sympathetic daughters gave each other a look that said, "It's going to be a long day."

"Let's try the mall," Brenda suggested. "With all of the stores there, I am sure you'll find something."

"I suppose," I said, turning around slowly.

"I want to get this first," Rachael said, lifting a dress with a black lace bodice and silk skirt dangling from a white hanger.

Together we all stood in the checkout line where I burst out suddenly, throwing my hands over my face. My daughters rushed to my side, putting their arms around my shoulders.

"Oh, Mom. It's going to be ok."

"A few weeks ago, your dad asked me if I wanted a diamond," I said between the sniffles. "I asked him what made him think that and he said he never got me a diamond, but he would if I wanted one. After I thought about it, I told him I had him and that was all I needed."

"That's sweet, Mom," Rachael said.

"I should have taken the diamond!" I laughed and soon my daughters and granddaughters laughed, too.

We headed over to the mall after Rachael made her purchase.

I weaved in and out of the racks at dressbarn, our first stop inside the mall. Color. Lots and lots of color. No purple. The girls tried to help, but I did not cooperate.

Feeling defeated and ready to give up, I started to leave when I spied a plain black dress on the clearance rack. I pulled the dress off the rack and headed into the dressing room. Once I had the dress on, I looked up and down at myself in the mirror. The scoop neckline and cap sleeves did not restrict my movement. The skirt, its hemline just below my knees, flowed nicely. Still unsure, I stepped out of the dressing room to get an opinion from my daughters.

Almost in unison the girls said, "Mom, that looks really nice. I think it's perfect."

The perfect dress had a red belt.

Red.

Checking the accessory display proved futile as far as finding a purple belt. However, a black scarf with stripes of turquoise, violet, and silver seemed just right to compliment a plain black dress. The turquoise and silver correlated nicely with the color in Willie's tie, connecting him and me. The violet satisfied my need for the color purple.

My daughters helped get me checked out. They cared for me like I had been afflicted with some disease. Oh wait. I had been. My heart had been broken and half of me no longer existed.

I was still in need of a purple belt, so we headed to Younkers. Thankfully, we located a belt quickly as fatigue began overtaking me. I needed to go home. The world looked as though it had no idea what had transpired. No idea that my sweetie no longer breathed.

The checkout line only had two customers and we lined up behind them. The cashier offered to provide information on the current sales events. I shifted my weight from one side to the other. Customer one listened intently, politely declined, paid for her purchases, and left.

Customer two had one item, a purse. This would be fast. After listening to the sales spiel, she pointed out a tiny imperfection on the purse. She wondered if they had any others as she just didn't know if she wanted it like that. She hemmed. She hawed. Obviously, she deemed this decision far more important than an act of God.

Shifting my weight again, I sighed . . . loudly. Unmistakably forlorn, I muttered, "Does she not realize just how trivial that purse is in the scheme of life?" Finally, she paid for the purse and moved on.

"I am not interested in your sales or anything else. I just want this belt." I stated. My girls, obviously embarrassed by me, remained silent. Clearly unhappy period, I paid for the belt, thankful that the time to go home had arrived.

When, if ever, would I feel alive again?

So the king asked me, "Why does your face look so sad when you are not ill? This can be nothing but sadness of heart." I was very much afraid. Nehemiah 2:2

Chapter 6

Final Words

"Bud, are you ready?" Rachael hollered up the stairs.

Monday morning. Willie's coronation service would take place this afternoon. The children, grandchildren, and I had to meet Jeane at the funeral home and finalize things before we met at the church. It would be the first time I had seen my husband since Bob and his assistant had taken him from our home five days earlier.

"Yeah. I'm coming," Bud said as he came down the stairs. "What do we have to do anyway?"

"I don't know, Bud. Jeane just asked that we all come," I said.

Once we arrived at Proko-Wall, Jeane directed us into the room where Willie lie in his casket. The sight of him took my breath away. He had that effect on me, especially when we had been apart for a few days. How handsome and peaceful he looked lying there in his suit.

The children had a hard time seeing their dad. In fact, Bud immediately left the room, but I went to Willie and touched his face, letting my hand linger there before I ran it over his hair. Though cold to the touch, he still warmed my heart.

His hands, folded over one another, held both his Green Bay Packers cap and my ponytail. Perfect. Then I noticed his ChapStick in his suit pocket. That had to be changed. Jeane came back to check on us.

"His ChapStick needs to be in his right front pants pocket, Jeane. Otherwise, he looks wonderful," I said.

"I'll change that for you," Jeane responded. "If everything else is okay, I'll see you at the church at one o'clock."

We headed out to the van to go home and prepare ourselves for the service later that day. "Do you have the eulogy done, Mom?" Rachael asked.

The eulogy is a speech that relates anecdotes about the deceased one's life. Our pastor had asked a few times about the eulogy. Our church secretary had mentioned it when I dropped off Willie's baptismal certificate for the bulletin.

A eulogy is usually delivered by a family friend or a close acquaintance. In the past, I had attended funerals where I had failed to say something, share a story or relate a special moment that I had experienced with the deceased. So much about my husband was dear to me. Not wanting those regrets again, I decided, even though unconventional, I'd deliver my husband's eulogy. I was his best friend.

Sleep evaded me for the most part, leaving me plenty of time to think about what I wanted to say. Different memories would weave in and out of my mind, much like the Zippin Pippin roller coaster goes up and down its track at Bay Beach Amusement Park. If the recollection included something I considered incorporating into the eulogy, I made a notation on a sheet of scratch paper. Piles of notes lay around the house—in the bedroom, the kitchen, the office, the living room. I thought about that man everywhere.

Our granddaughter, Jasmine, wanted to make a PowerPoint presentation for her grandpa's funeral service. After confirming this being a possibility with Pastor Dave, Jasmine went right to work. Not only would this help her heal, but it would also give me the support I needed during the delivery of the eulogy.

She and I became a team, plotting and planning together to make this all work for the both of us. Excitedly, she suggested having our very own signal so everything would flow along. God provided me strength through this little girl, not typically the place one would look for that kind of power, but I found it there all the same.

"Mom? Did you hear me?" Rachael asked.

"I jotted down some things I want to say," I told her.

"No, Mom. Do you have it written out?" she asked emphatically.

"I just wrote down little phrases to help me remember. It'll be ok." I attempted to reassure her.

"Mom. If Pastor Dave is going to save you if you can't go on, those little phrases won't mean anything to him. You have to have it written out."

I felt like a scolded child.

"I guess I never thought about that," I answered quietly.

So home I went to write out the eulogy that I had played over and over again in my head.

It is God who arms me with strength and makes my way perfect. 2 Samuel 22:33

The Coronation Service

I could see dark circles under my eyes as I looked at myself in the mirror, telltale signs that I lacked sleep. I found a tube of concealer inside the medicine cabinet and began applying it under my eyes. I let out a loud sigh. The concealer didn't conceal and I hadn't awakened from this nightmare.

Rummaging through the basket of makeup proved successful in locating a tube of candy apple red lipstick. It slid easily over my lips and I hoped it would distract people from my sad eyes. After I finished dressing, I found my kids ready and waiting to drive me to the church.

At the church, we found the funeral home staff busy finishing up preparations for the service. My sweetie's picture sat on the table outside the narthex doors, and it warmed my heart to see the cast iron Dutch oven on the matting. Willie would be pleased. A garden stone rested on a stand on the same table with a tag attached indicating the friends who had sent it. How thoughtful. Love overwhelmed me.

Passing through the doors into the narthex, I intended to help the kids place the mementos we had brought with us when I saw my husband at the front of the church. My heart gave pause and I put down the box I held as a strong urge propelled me to him. My steps, slow and precise, led me on the ecru Berber carpet, up the aisle between the rows of natural pine pews. If one could not see my destination, they might think I auditioned for a role. However, the role I had today no one could prepare me for.

When I reached the casket, I ran my hand over it. Everything just as we had ordered. I looked at my husband. So handsome. So at peace. Though you couldn't see it by looking, he had a heart of gold.

"Well, you finally beat me to church, Sweetie. That's a first," I said.

Stepping back, I noticed the urn sitting near the foot of the casket and the garden stone on a stand at the head of it. To the right, the DVD player projected photos of Willie on a giant screen. Autumn-colored flowers adorned the remaining areas on either end of the casket. I read the cards.

"Oh darling. Do you know how much we are loved?" My empty, aching heart nearly burst.

Heading back to the narthex of the church, I planned to check on things. The mementos—a cast iron skillet, a salesman sample stove, a refinished shipping crate—had been displayed next to a photograph of Willie and me and his service picture. The picture boards, containing so many precious memories, stood like sentries on easels. Everything so reminiscent of him and though far away, I sensed him close.

The two o'clock hour neared and people started coming into the church. One of the first couples to arrive were our elderly friends, both nearly 90. They moved slowly, and not just because of their kyphotic postures and canes. Their hearts ached for my family and me. She clutched my arm as we walked up the aisle toward the casket. He took a moment to talk to Bud.

She held my hand as we stood beside the casket reminiscing. Soon, her husband joined us. They moved on and someone else waited to take their spot, and so the afternoon went. My intention had not been to stand next to the casket of my husband during the visitation. *How did I end up here?*

Even though already in God's loving arms, God continued to use Willie to provide me with the courage and strength I would need to get through the afternoon. Standing there next to his casket, I could reach out and hold his hand as I had done for nearly thirty years. I laughed at myself. If it had been someone else, I would think touching a corpse creepy. But this was my sweetie . . .

The line grew long, spanning the length of the church aisle and right out the door. The pews filled up, too, and I became overwhelmed by the presence of all the loved ones. Sometimes we don't realize how many blessings we have in life until they gather in one place. In a moment of sorrow, I could still see God's good work in my life.

Rachael brought me a stool and a cold glass of water. "Mom. You need to sit down before you collapse." Gently, but firmly, she guided me onto the seat.

I sipped the water. As good as it tasted, nausea plagued my empty stomach. Sitting did not last long. I found it difficult to talk to people when I had to look up at them. Besides, my weak body needed Willie to lean on.

Jeane, the funeral director, came and whispered firmly in my ear. "Move the line along." The four o'clock hour neared and people still wound out the door. Visitors continued to offer condolences. I quickly thanked each one for coming. We shared hugs and before I knew it, four o'clock arrived and Jeane reappeared, guiding me and my family out of the sanctuary. The ceremony needed to commence so everyone still in line had to find a place to sit.

Jeane spoke softly to us. "After everyone is seated, I'll take you back out for your final goodbyes. After that, you'll all meet in the sacristy for a quick review of the service with the pastor. Are you doing okay?" Jeane gently touched my arm. I nodded.

With everyone seated, we gathered around the casket for our final goodbyes. We stood strong together, hand in hand, knowing we would never again lay our eyes upon Willie's physical body. Husband, father, grandfather. He was all these things to us and much more. Numbness kept the tears at bay.

We filed into the sacristy while they closed the casket for the service. Pastor Dave accompanied us as well as my brother-in-law, David, who agreed to read both the Old Testament and Epistle passages for the service. We began a quick review of the service and who was doing what.

"Will someone be doing a eulogy?" Pastor Dave asked.

"Yes. I am," I responded.

"Debbi, you are doing the eulogy?" he questioned. Though I couldn't see his face, I could sense the eyebrows raised.

I assured him I needed to do it. "Besides, I have it all typed up so you can save me if I can't go on." He seemed relieved. So did I.

Comfort also came in the form of the PowerPoint presentation Jasmine had prepared for the eulogy. The morning had been long in attempting to get the computer's cooperation, but now they assured me it was set to go. My son, my daughter, my brothers, and my granddaughter had all been diligently working to get the computer to cooperate. Fears surfaced that it wouldn't be available for the service even though I desperately needed both the PowerPoint show and Jasmine. *Thank you, God.*

After taking a deep breath, I silently asked God to provide me with the strength I would need to get through the service. The time to begin had arrived.

"Amazing Grace" began to play and the beautiful voices and John could be heard as we filed into the church. The family headed for the second pew and Pastor Dave took the three steps up to the chancel. When the song finished, he said a few welcoming words before leading the opening prayer.

Then the moment I both feared and longed for. He called me to the lectern to do the eulogy.

Jasmine and I nodded at one another in the pew. As we stood, she took my hand and leaned in close to me. "We don't have a signal," she stated anxiously.

"It's okay, kiddo. We'll make it work," I said, reassuring her as much as myself.

She headed to the computer and I stepped up to the lectern. First, I thanked Pastor Dave and then addressed everyone in attendance. "Pastor Dave didn't tell me I had a time limit." The laughter lightened the mood, but I still avoided making eye contact with anyone. I knew that would surely lead to my demise.

When preparing the eulogy, I divided it into sections. In Jasmine's PowerPoint, she put photos together to match each section. Each time I came to the end of a section, I smiled and nodded at Jasmine and she moved on to the next slide. Some humor had been injected into the eulogy as my husband loved a good joke. When we finished, I think everyone knew how much we loved Willie. Stepping down the three steps, I met Jasmine and we walked back together. My legs, weak again, caused me to collapse in the pew.

My brother-in-law stepped up to the lectern to read God's word. I noted an unsteadiness in his voice, especially as he read the Epistle. He must be recalling how much Willie's earthly body caused him to groan. David returned to the pew and Pastor Dave read the Gospel passage.

Following the readings, Jennifer and John joined the congregation in singing "The Old Rugged Cross." Never had it sounded so exquisite. Never had the words meant so much.

When they finished, Pastor Dave stepped behind the casket for a sermon that melded together stories about Willie, the scripture readings, and the purpose in our gathering. An animated speaker, he spoke with such passion. Willie's confirmation, his service to our country, his roles in the family, all came to life for us. He spoke of the journey my husband had begun and the gift of eternal life our Savior has given. The sermon concluded with a congregational reciting of the Apostle's Creed.

The melodious voices of Jennifer and John sang "Just a Closer Walk with Thee" prior to the closing prayers. How fortunate for Willie that he indeed walked closer to thee. The thought comforted me. In unison, the crowd recited The Lord's Prayer and began the recessional hymn, "Softly and Tenderly Jesus is Calling."

The pallbearers, my brothers, brother-in-law, and cousin-in-law, moved to the front of the church. Dividing into groups of two, they took their places on either side of the casket and began walking down the aisle with my husband. The immediate family followed the casket, and then one by one the people in the pews joined the procession. The casket and the pallbearers went down the elevator while the rest of us took the stairs to exit through the front doors of the church.

We gathered there outside the church doors. The hearse, parked off to the right, sat with the casket approximately ten feet behind it. I stood next to my children and grandchildren while the rest of our family and friends gathered around us. Once everyone had gotten outside, the three-man honor guard team each fired three rifle volleys. Though we all expected it, our bodies jumped at the sound.

The flag detail precisely folded the United States flag that had been draped over my husband's casket. One of the men presented me with the flag. *How am I supposed to accept this? I want to dignify my husband.*

"Thank you for the service your husband gave to his country. I want you to know that each one of us here today are Vietnam veterans."

Another unexpected blessing.

The pallbearers moved back to the casket, guiding it into the hearse. The funeral home staff closed the door. Standing together, we all watched as the hearse slowly drove away.

The tears flowed. I raised my hand as if to reach out and touch Willie, to place my palm to his as I had done so many times before.

"Bye Sweetie. I love you. You know I do."

> *Blessed are those who mourn, for they will be comforted.*
> *Matthew 5:4*

Chapter 7

Sympathy Cards:
My Cup Runneth Over

Willie passed away on Thursday morning and Friday's mail already included a handful of sympathy cards. The envelopes had not been opened, but they didn't need to be to reveal the contents. The house had been a bustle of activity, not allowing me the time I wanted to devote to the kindnesses that I knew they contained.

Or perhaps, by not opening them, going to sleep, and waking up again, I could start the week over.

That hadn't happened.

There had been so much to do and little time to do it so each day, I added the mail to the top of the ever growing pile on the kitchen table. Perhaps one morning at 3 a.m. when the rest of the world slept, I could look through the cards and find comfort. My heart ached and the tears did not cease to flow.

***

The morning following the funeral, Rachael arrived bright and early. Sleep continued to evade me, leaving me exhausted, and I did not rise to greet her. She attempted to involve me in some activity.

"They are bringing the things from the funeral home sometime this morning," I said in a monotone voice as I stared out the window. Ah, my excuse to continue to mope around the house and avoid engaging in any productive pursuit.

Several hours later, following a phone call to the funeral home, the flowers, cards, guest book, and other things arrived, delivered by strangers. Jeane had the day off. She had worked all weekend on my husband's send-off.

My pleasure in having the items home did not reveal itself through my somber expression. Standing aside, I watched as the strangers moved in and out the front door. Once everything had been brought in, I thanked them, bidding them farewell as I shut the door. Turning back around, I saw my quaint house filled to the brim. I began reading all the cards on the flowers circling the room as though I'd never seen them before.

"Mom, why don't we look at these cards? There are quite a few here and you have that basketful on the table." Rachael struggled to occupy my mind.

"I suppose," I said, collapsing on the floor in front of the black leather loveseat, curling my knees up to my chest, wrapping my arms around them, and resting my head.

Make the world go away.

Rachael went to get the other cards. She returned with them, a letter opener, a pad of paper, and a pen. "I'll make a list so you know who sent what."

She sat the basket of cards on the coffee crate coffee table and curled her leg up underneath her as she sat down on the couch, poised to take notes as though she had suddenly become my personal secretary.

I sighed. "That's a good idea." After lifting my head, I pulled a card off the top of the pile.

The lightweight letter opener seemed heavy today, requiring much energy to use. After sliding the opener across the top edge, I battled with the envelope to remove its contents. My bare hands struggled like I had donned a pair of overstuffed gloves.

Why can't anything be easy?

As silent tears rolled endlessly down my cheeks, I read the cards aloud. Between making notations, Rachael would hand me another tissue.

A bevy of beautiful cards shared a common theme. Time, friends, family, and God would heal us from our loss. Many of them encouraged us to hang onto the memories we shared. Personal notes confessed to not understanding and offers to do whatever we needed. Many wished to share hugs which I fully intended to collect later. It had not been a week and I already missed the hugs!

When I came to the card from my brother and sister-in-law, I stopped briefly. The front of the card pictured a sundial very similar to the one on the urn. How had they known?

Many of the cards contained enclosures. Scripture verses gave hope. Short stories recounted tales of survival. Poems embraced the feelings in my heart. Several included checks or cash in memory of my beloved.

Upon opening the next card, I discovered three neatly folded one dollar bills, a gift from one of my senior friends who had long ago been widowed. Pausing then, I held both the card and the money up to my chest.

Over and over I had read "God is with you," but now I heard it clearly. Remembering the widow Jesus had seen give her small monetary gift to the church, all she had, told me God had not abandoned me.

As he looked up, Jesus saw the rich putting their gifts into the temple treasury. He also saw a poor widow put in two very small copper coins. "I tell you the truth," he said, "this poor widow has put in more than all the others. All these people gave their gifts out of their wealth; but she out of her poverty put in all she had to live on." Luke 21:1-4

Healing Garden

"Mom?" my daughter called over the whine of the front door closing.

"In here," I yelled as I tossed the brown and tan damask print quilt aside so I could sit up on the edge of the bed. I turned the clock radio toward me. Illuminated yellow numbers boldly proclaimed 8:08. Ugh.

How busy making all the arrangements had kept me. The coronation service, the funeral, had been two days ago. Now most of the phone calls had ceased and visitors had returned to their own lives. Yes, other lives went on even though I felt mine had stopped. Other lives, except apparently my children's.

While I appreciated their thoughtfulness, I longed to be alone, to just lie in bed and cry, to make the world go away. However, each time I'd get out of bed, I'd find one of them there, hovering. I know they worried about their mom, but I really wanted to scream and cry. Some way, somehow I needed to get my frustrations out.

In the living room, amid vases of cut zinnias, orange-dyed carnations, and cattails and pots of philodendrons and chrysanthemums, my daughter, Rachael, sat on the black leather couch and my son, Bud, in his over-stuffed recliner. I sat sideways in a corner of the loveseat, my bent legs wrapped in my arms, my head rotated left and resting on my knees. Through the window, I could see the bright sun. It did not betray the beauty of the Indian summer day. Inside, I yearned for that beauty, that peacefulness.

After some fragile silence, I lifted my head. "Should we go out and dig the memorial garden?" I suggested.

Of course, my son and daughter who had no interest in gardening jumped at the opportunity to go out and dig up the yard. Though they nodded their heads in agreement, a glance between them sarcastically said, "Sure." They continued to tread lightly where their mother was concerned.

We walked around the yard first, as I had not really decided where to put the memorial garden.

"What about here by the wagon wheels, Mom? Dad got them for you and he always liked it under this shade tree," Bud asked.

"No," I said, emphasizing the words with a subtle shake of my head.

"We could put it here in this corner," Rachael suggested, sweeping her arm as though she just revealed the prize behind door number one.

"Mmm. I don't think so," I said. I pressed my lips together, pulling down the left corner of my mouth as I pondered the location. I did not want to rush into just any area. This would be where the garden urn containing Willie's ashes would be located. I wanted to see it from anywhere.

We continued to stroll the border of the backyard and I continued to veto the children's suggestions. The air felt good, only a faint breeze, and that offered solace. The autumn grass felt soft underfoot, reveling in surviving the summer's heat, I suppose. I longed to hear a bird's song, the scurry of a squirrel's paws along the wooden pickets of the neighbor's fence, the rustle of browned daylily leaves as a rabbit took cover.

I longed to hear signs of life.

I headed toward the garage and the children followed. There we sat on the flowered cushions of the swing in silence, scanning one side of the yard, then the other. Orange ditch lilies stood like sentries along the back of the house. Black bears played leap frog between the garden shed and the playhouse. Dried iris leaves waved discreetly from the rear of the playhouse. I stood up. The kids followed.

While walking to an area by the playhouse, I said, "I think I want it here." I turned around and stopped. The kids glanced at one another, opening their eyes wide in silent conversation.

"It's more or less a central location in the yard. I would be able to see the urn whether working in the garden or in the house doing the dishes."

Willie had built the playhouse for our granddaughters ten years earlier. Beehive yellow paint covered the six by six-foot structure. The trim around the windows, door, and the railed porch bore a bright cerulean blue. A flowered knob in princess pink allowed access through the grapevine wreath adorned door. Willie enjoyed watching children enter and exit that door, smiles on their faces. It would bring me peace to have his garden there.

Relieved that I had finally made a firm decision on the site, Bud headed to the garden shed for the shovel. When he returned, he stood, shovel in hand and that dumbfounded look on his face, the one he used when he wanted to dig up the yard as much as his dad liked me digging up the yard.

"Umm? Do you want me to dig here, Mom? Or here? I'm not exactly sure where you want this?"

I reached for the green-handled shovel and dug an outline. Rachael and Bud knelt on the ground and began freeing the soil, removing the tufts of grass to create a smooth bed for planting. I noted their silent conversation continued, their cautious movement. Did they still fear my sanity had been lost? Or perhaps their enthusiasm for gardening was being expressed in the slowness of activity. Nevertheless, I saw an opportunity for myself there.

"Do you and Bud want to go and get some crescent stones for the edging?" I asked as I walked the perimeter of the garden to estimate how many stones we would need. My daughter offered to go alone. "No. Take your brother to help you," I said.

"But Mom . . . Are you sure? I don't want to leave you alone," Rachael pleaded.

"I'll be fine. Get the gray ones to set it apart from the other gardens," I said. I did want to set it apart, but truly, I thought the color matched the depression I felt as a young woman whose husband had died.

Off they went to Menards. Finally, for the first time since Willie had passed away, I was free to lose my mind.

Jamming the shovel forcefully into the ground, I heaved one shovelful of sod and then another into the blue Union wheelbarrow. I screamed, "Darn you darling! I was not ready for you to go! I don't want to be alone! I hate being alone! I hate sleeping alone! I hate waking up alone! I wanted to get used to you dropping me off at work and picking me up!

"I don't want to be without you!"

I exerted more force. Dirt flew like soda from a shaken bottle. My breathing became as labored as the physical work I engaged in.

"Just so you know, Sweetie, I am STILL digging up the yard!"

The shovel flew from my hands like an eagle attacking prey. I fell to my knees, collapsed back on my legs, and cradled my face in my dirty hands. Loud, long cries surged from somewhere deep inside. Tears spilled down my cheeks, leaving trails through the dirt that had settled there. I laid down on the ground next to the freshly turned soiled, longing for the impossible: to lie next to Willie.

Unaware of how much time had passed, I eventually got myself up off the ground and finished removing the grass from the memorial garden. The tufts of grass, shaken violently to remove the soil bound to their roots, were forcefully tossed into a galvanized tub. At last, the area before me boasted a dark brown canvas of unplanted soil.

Standing and dusting myself off, I returned to sitting on the swing, still all alone. Silent now, I listened and found the neighborhood quiet. No sirens sounded, so my neighbors either hadn't been home or I scared them into going inside and locking their doors.

I could feel and hear the pounding of my heart. I experienced some relief as I sat there alone. Aunt Estell always said gardening was good for the soul, and never had I felt that more than now. When my children returned with the gray crescent stones, I did my best to appear completely normal.

Once the stones had been unloaded, Rachael and Bud began positioning them while I planted the mums I had received at the funeral service. I planted the two identical yellow and orange ones on either side of the site for the urn. To the left of one, I placed the burgundy flowered plant and to the right of the other, a smaller, russet-colored one. Normally, I enjoyed the beautiful, bountiful flowers of the chrysanthemums. Today, they only spoke of grief.

I walked away from the garden and went to the house. Just inside the backdoor, I grabbed Willie's work boots. I returned and sat them between the flowers on the left side. I departed again, this time heading to the garden shed. When I came back, I placed a rake, a cast-off piece of farm equipment Willie had brought home for me, between the flowers on the right side. Willie grew up on a farm, so it seemed ideal for his garden. A watering can decorated with a scarecrow, a traditional fall decoration, took up residence next to the five-pronged rake.

I went to the front of the playhouse, pulled out the stake of the coffee house bird house Willie and I had picked up when we traveled to Iowa, and moved it behind the mums on the left. I managed a smile. We loved coffee and the little coffee house in Cedar Rapids.

Back in the garden shed, I pulled out a second-hand, cast iron kettle Willie had just given me for my flea market gardening. A memorial garden wouldn't be complete for my sweetie if it did not contain at least one piece of cast iron. I sat it to the far left.

Finally, we placed two stones, a small gray and yellow one that said "With God all things are possible," and the one we had selected at the funeral home that said "No farewell words were spoken, No time to say good-bye, You were gone before we knew it, And only God knows why," on the freshly turned soil.

We stood up, wiping the dirt from our hands as we stared at the garden. Everything looked fresh and peaceful. Everything said fall and change, endings and beginnings. Everything spoke of the man we all loved.

We sat together on the swing, Rachael, Bud, and me, admiring our handiwork. Today's therapy had been completed.

Where has your lover gone, most beautiful of women? Which way did your lover turn, that we may look for him with you? My lover has gone down to his garden, to the beds of spices, to browse in the gardens and to gather lilies. I am my lover's and my lover is mine; he browses among the lilies. Song of Songs 6:1-3

The Homecoming

Walking back and forth across the floor, I checked the clock each time I turned around as though my pacing would make time go faster. I anxiously peered out the front window. *What kept him?* My breaths became deep and labored, my muscles tensed, and a numb sensation coursed through my body.

When I received the phone call, I had mixed emotions. Most women would be happy to hear about their husband's homecoming, but I had a pretty good idea how the wives of deceased servicemen felt. Even when I viewed those homecomings on a movie, I shed tears. The tears I shed now did not fall for a movie character.

Our youngest daughter repositioned herself on the couch as she laughed at the movie she and her little brother watched. Patting the seat next to her, she said, "Mom, why don't you sit down and watch this with us?"

"No, I can't. Jeane called and your dad is coming home today." I wrung my hands as I spoke, unable to hide my anxiety. Rachael and Bud looked at one another, unsure of what to do or say.

The day, perfect for a homecoming, started with the sun shining brightly and moderate temperatures. A mild breeze rustled the leaves that had already taken up residence on the lawn. Inside, however, I could sense an imminent storm. Dark clouds lingered and the wind churned. It would be another bittersweet moment, something I longed for but wished it would occur in a different way. My deepest desire, to have my husband home, wouldn't come in the manner I longed for, him driving his black Dodge Ram pickup with the stereo blaring. His arrival today would be much more low-key.

I caught a glimpse of the sun reflecting off a vehicle out of the corner of my eye, so I turned back around. The moment I had been anticipating had arrived. Jeane opened the back hatch, but I didn't wait for her to get the urn and knock. I swung open the front door and waited patiently, silently watching as she carried the urn up the sidewalk. Slowly, tears ran down my cheeks and that hollow feeling deepened.

Jeane handled the urn with care, knowing the importance of the contents. Taking the square of bubble wrap she had handed me, I placed it on the wooden floor in the corner of the living room to protect the floor. For now, Willie's urn could sit by the family quilt. The time was not right to put him in the garden.

Gently, I ran my fingertips over the engraving on the name plate. Touch had become such an important sense to me. My index finger lingered over his name. How precious this man was to me. That emptiness inside intensified. The tears flowed more freely.

Willie had come home.

And provide for those who grieve in Zion—to bestow on them a crown of beauty instead of ashes, the oil of gladness instead of mourning, and a garment of praise instead of a spirit of despair. They will be called oaks of righteousness, a planting of the LORD for the display of his splendor. Isaiah 61:3

Part Two

Grinding Gears

Tears Fall (For My Sweetie)

A month has passed since you left my side
Many days and nights to lay and cry
Tears fall without warning so often
But the heartache I feel doesn't soften
I cry in the morning when I wake
It's hard to smile when your heart aches
No one to fix the crossword mistakes
No one to tease me for heaven's sake
The tears they fall through the day
When you don't hold my hand and say
I love you sweetie in every way
They fall at night when alone in bed I lay
When I'm in church and kneel to pray
When I'm at home or gone away
You gave me strength and believed in me
Now emptiness is what I feel, what I see
The tears I cry are not for you
You're dancing in heaven without any shoes
The tears I cry I shed for me
A life without you is one I didn't see.

Chapter 8

Captain's Log

"**O**h, Sweetie. I need to talk to you. You've taught me so much, celebrated with me when we triumphed, and held me when we struggled."

I stared at the white swirls on the ceiling as I lie in bed. "Yes, I know we had our share of battles, too, but when things got heated, I could always persuade you to see things my way." I managed a smile.

I rolled over and pulled his pillow close to me. The faint scent of Jovan musk lingered there. "Lord, I could always count on him. My rock. My best friend. You know how my heart aches without him. Isn't there some way I can talk to him?"

At no time did I ever need to talk to Willie more than I did right now. I was confronting things I had no idea how to handle.

On that dreadful October day when my journey began, I talked to Willie out loud as I laid in our bed, fighting tears and fighting with our pillows. Walking through our empty house, all hours of the day and night, I consulted with him about what I was supposed to do. Strolling our gardens, I chatted with him. Sitting on the backyard swing where we had solved the world's problems, I begged him to listen to me. As crazy as it had made me, I would have given anything to hear him ask, "What?"

I could hear the Lord reminding me of the gifts He blessed me with. I started keeping a diary in sixth grade, and I continued to express myself in written words off and on throughout my life. Somewhere along the line it became known as journaling, and regardless of the title, it helped me cope with life.

A blank journal awaited my pen and I took full advantage of it. It would be my captain's log, where I could talk freely to Willie.

The theme song from *Star Trek* played in my head and I smiled. Willie loved that television show and a *Star Trek* movie had been one of the first movies we went to together. A captain's log seemed the perfect solution for my conversations with him.

I opened the leather-bound cover and flipped to the first page. Carefully, I wrote the date in the upper right hand corner:

November 1, 2012

"Hey Sweetie, It's been two weeks today since God eased your pain and my heartache began. I don't think this empty feeling will ever go away. You completed me and now I am a puzzle with a piece missing. I went back to work on Tuesday and it's been tough. My class participants, my co-workers, my patients have all been wonderful, but no one can fill my void."

When I made the next entry, I added the time next to the date: 4:30 a.m.

"Hey Sweetie. Sleep is hard to come by these days. There is no warm body next to me when my feet get cold. I still feel so empty, darling. I just want you back here with me. There is so much to deal with and I need your strength.

When I left for work yesterday, it really hit me hard when I turned off our bedroom light and you weren't lying there in our bed. That set me up for a big meltdown to start my day at work. It's so hard to lose your best friend and not ache so much.

I am Humpty Dumpty and no one can put me back together again."

Journaling not only helped me talk to Willie, but it also permitted me to express the turmoil that went on inside me. The areas that I needed to take to God in prayer revealed themselves. Strength became a frequent request. Memories evoked as I continued to record my thoughts and feelings. Journaling allowed me to discover things to be thankful for. I let God know that, too.

"Dear Lord, let me know I am making progress on this road I travel. I am afraid. I never imagined life without him. Let me know, even though Willie has gone ahead, that I am not alone. That You are accompanying me."

I clicked the lamp's switch off and instantly the room became dark. I could not even cry myself to sleep.

> *It is God who arms me with strength and makes my way perfect. 2 Samuel 22:33*

November 8, 2012, 10:03 p.m.

I have had a busy day. Back to the lawyer's office again. More papers to sign. To the VA. They were very nice there. And now I am here, missing you. I can't believe I am not going to take any more trips with you, hold you in my arms or be held in yours. I miss you terrible, darling, and I must pray for strength every day.

It helps if I imagine you dancing in heaven. First, you were my dance partner and then I had to share you with the kids and the grandkids, but no worries. It made me love you even more. What will I do without you? We never even said goodbye.

Save a dance for me.

Red Tape

The amber light flashed frantically, cautioning me to empty the bin. I sighed as I eyed the paper stacks around me. It appeared that I had not even begun and I had been shredding for what seemed like hours. The bin slid out easily so it could be emptied. Though lightweight, I struggled as if it had been filled with river rock. If ever there was a reason for going paperless, it was the death of a loved one.

Once the bin was replaced and the amber light glowed steady, I laid down on the carpet, staring up at the swirls on the white ceiling. The list of items requested by the attorney's office passed through my mind—wills, titles, deeds, certificates. If it had been "joint," I needed it. Had been. The words haunted me. Closing my eyes, I let the tears stream from them right into my ears.

Time dragged ever so slowly, so it surprised me to see a few minutes had actually been an hour. I sat myself up again and reached for another stack of papers; mail that I had no desire to open, so I had just let it pile up. Unopened mail that somehow would hold reality at bay until I decided to let it be. Funny how one can be deceived into feeling so powerful when they are so powerless.

Sighing, I slid the metal letter opener across the top of the business-size envelope. The sight of another pink envelope caused me to exhale deeply. If only a pink envelope meant I was dismissed from my position, I would be in good shape. A pink slip from being alone would be most welcome. But no such luck. It merely meant I let something else go too long.

Setting the letter aside, I reached for another envelope. So far so good. No pink envelope. The contents, pulled out and unfolded, revealed bulky red letters stamped askew at the top of the paper, boldly stating its message: PAST DUE. I crumpled up the contents and tossed them across the room.

Assuming it to be safer, I reached for an envelope from the medical insurance company. I expected an explanation of benefits inside, giving me peace of mind. A fight ensued with the letter opener as it had caught on something on the envelope. Such frustration over an everyday task. Once I could access the contents, I confirmed my theory: an explanation of benefits. Total benefits paid for this claim: zero dollars and zero cents. Apparently, my husband did not need an ambulance.

Tears stung my eyes. A pit formed in the bottom of my stomach. My head ached. Concentrating seemed a challenging task and I wondered how I would get through the day, let alone the rest of my life. Dropping the letter on the floor, I headed back to bed where perhaps the world would go away.

Several days passed before I could return to the paperwork. Praying for God's guidance, I picked up the phone and called the ambulance service. To my surprise, a compassionate woman answered.

"I'm calling about my husband's rescue squad bill. Payment has been denied by the insurance company. I don't feel I was qualified to determine whether he needed an ambulance or not," I said.

Mary confirmed name, date of service, my husband's birth date. "I am so sorry for your loss. Let me resubmit the claim with a letter explaining the circumstances," she said.

Graciously, I accepted her proposal, but I could sense God directing me to plead for myself as well.

"Dear Lord, I know what you want me to do, but you must give me the words to say. Only you are aware of what needs to be said and how. Please guide me."

I wrote out a check to the ambulance service before sitting down at the computer, where the words flowed easily. God indeed provided me with the terminology required. Once completed, I dropped both the check to the ambulance service and the letter to the insurance company in the mailbox.

Rachael had arrived by that time, as she had offered to accompany me to have Willie's cell phone turned off. I donned my coat, grabbed my purse and we left the house. We found the small cell phone store void of people except for the two clerks who sat behind the counter. The heavier of the two hobbled out from behind the counter to assist us.

"I need to have this cell phone turned off," I said.

"Oh, you don't want to do that. You have the best plan available, and if you need to turn it on again, you'll have to pay for a new plan," the clerk said.

"Yes, I do want to shut it off," I responded.

"If you shut it off . . ."

I interrupted him. "My husband has a plan with unlimited minutes and the rates are out of this world. I want to shut the phone off," I said firmly. Why do people think they know what is best when they don't even know the circumstances?

My daughter leaned in close to the salesclerk. "My dad has passed away. Just shut the phone off."

He completed the task silently, finishing up by asking me for a signature. Leaving the shop, I felt numb. The phone had not been the only thing cut off.

Over the next few months, for the most part, I was able to rid the mail of pink envelopes and bulky red words. I reluctantly learned to live without my husband's assistance and income. Fortunately, Willie had seen to it that we had both an attorney and a financial advisor prior to his death, experts who advised me throughout the process.

Nearly four months after sending the letter regarding the ambulance bill, I began opening letters from the insurance company again. (I still had not surpassed piling up the mail.) One of those envelopes contained a check for the full amount of the rescue squad bill. "Thank you, God!" I exclaimed out loud.

I turned the envelope over and checked the postmark. It had arrived nearly two and a half months ago. I smiled. Sometimes, it pays to open the mail.

"How you have helped the powerless! How you have saved the arm that is feeble! Job 26:2

November 9, 2012, 11:32 p.m.

The pain you suffered here on earth—your knees, your shoulders, your wrist— it's gone and at last you've found peace. Help me to find it, too.

November 10, 2012, 3:47 a.m.

Oh, how I wish you were here to talk to. I sure could use your arms around me. Sometimes, that's all I needed to feel better. I miss you, Sweetie. Without you, I am empty. I never knew how much my heart could break . . .

November 11, 2012, 5 a.m.

Good morning, Sweetie. It's Sunday morning and I am going to church again. I won't sit up front though. That nearly crushed me last week. I needed you beside me and you just weren't there. Love you bunches.

The Crying Room

I eased the van into the parking space directly under the light and turned off the ignition. I sighed as I placed my folded hands on top of the steering wheel and peered through the windows, where I noted little activity.

C'mon. You can do this. My chest rose and fell slowly under my sweatshirt, but my heart raced.

It's only milk. Just a single gallon. My breathing became labored. *In the door. Down one aisle. Back again. You can do this.*

I reached for the door handle, opened the door, and slid out of the van slowly. One step, two . . . fifteen. I passed through the automatic

75

doors. Bright fluorescent bulbs reflected off polished floor tiling. Macintosh apples piled high to my left didn't tempt me. Greenish yellow bananas stacked on artificial turf greeted me as I rounded the corner. I worked my way past semi-ripe tomatoes and deep green avocados. I picked up the pace.

I'm going to make it. Just focus.

As I rounded the pallets holding boxed cereal and red and white sale signs, mere feet away from the cooler of milk, I felt as though someone sideswiped me.

No-o-o-o. It can't be.

Tears gushed forth, and even if they had not been silent, I would still hear the words Elton John crooned from the overhead speakers.

"Sad Songs." Our song.

If Willie had been there, he'd dance with me right in the aisle. I closed my eyes and I could see that roguish smile.

"C'mon," he'd say as he pulled me close. "This is our song." He'd twirl me around, wrap me in his arms, and kiss me gently. "I love you, Sweetie," he'd say. And, I'd love him, too.

Biting my lower lip did nothing to control the tears, so my vision was as clear as when I went without my glasses. The gallon of milk, the aisle to the checkout became hazy shapes, but somehow I made it.

The cashier scanned the milk and I failed miserably at avoiding eye contact. She walked around the register and placed her hand on my shoulder. "Honey, are you okay? Can I call someone for you?" Her words broke the dam I had tried to build.

"I just need to pay for my milk. I'll be fine." I shook my head emphatically.

God, make the world go away.

"I can call someone for you," she pleaded.

"I just miss my husband. No one can help me with that," I said.

Once the milk had been paid for, the cashier squeezed my hand. "I'll pray for you."

Back in the van, I popped the "Romantic Getaway" CD into the player. The kids helped me create the disc when I surprised Willie with a weekend away to Milwaukee. After fast-forwarding to track three, I leaned my head into the headrest and danced with Willie to our song.

* * *

Abundant tears. Anytime, anyplace they would lay in wait for me. Something would waylay me and down they'd come, sometimes flowing heavy like a fire hydrant being flushed; other times quietly trickling down my cheeks like a soaker hose. I had lost all control.

"Time to regain control," I said to my mirrored image as I hooked the delicate gold chain around my neck and then clasped the ornate cross in my hand. "It's the last one you bought me, Sweetie," I said to Willie's portrait. "Wearing it makes me feel like you're with me at church. It's been nearly a month now and I am still going to church alone. The kids don't understand how I can go after what happened to you. I don't know how I can't.

"I'm trying out different pews, but I haven't found one that keeps me from crying yet. You know how much I hate people leaving the sanctuary during the service? Well, that would be me, going to dry my eyes. And if the praise band sings another one of our favorite hymns today, I'm probably going to scream right there on the spot.

"Last week, I could smell coconut shampoo and two weeks before, it was Jovan musk. These parishioners are killing me and they don't even know it." I closed my eyes and shook my head. "Wish me luck, Sweetie."

* * *

Not long after I arrived home from church, Rachael and my granddaughter, Jasmine, came through the backdoor.

"Hey, Mama. How are you doing today?" Rachael inquired as she put her arms around my shoulders and gave me a hug.

I shook my head. "Do you want to guess what Pastor Greg preached on today? 2 Corinthians 5:1-5. The same words I had read at your dad's service. It had me crying so much, I couldn't even sing half the hymns." I tilted my head to the left and rubbed my forehead with my fingertips. "I just don't foresee these tears stopping."

"It'll get easier, Mom. Just give it time," Rachael said, emphasizing the words with sympathetic blue eyes.

"I'm not so sure about that. The other night at the grocery store, the poor cashier offered to get me some help." I sighed, choking back the tears. "And going to work is a real killer. I cry all the way there and pray the tears will dry up by the time I have to walk in. How can I help people if it looks like I can't help myself?" I pulled another tissue from the box.

"I don't know what I am going to do." I wiped my eyes and my cheeks before running the tissue under my chin.

"I'm sorry, Mom," Rachael said. "I know you need to go grocery shopping and to work, and I know going to church is important to you. How did everything else go this morning?"

"Well, let's see. The pastor included those who mourn the loss of a loved one in the prayers and then . . ." I laughed nervously. "I went out to get my coat on and some woman tapped me on the shoulder. I don't have any idea who she is. When I turned around, she gave me a hug and said, 'I think you needed that.' I thanked her, but the tears just kept coming. What am I going to do? I don't want to stop going to church." I reached for another tissue.

Jasmine, who had been silent, came over and stood beside me. As she slid her arms around my neck and leaned her head into mine, she said. "Don't worry, Grandma. There's a crying room at church."

I tell you the truth, you will weep and mourn while the world rejoices. You will grieve, but your grief will turn to joy. So with you: Now is your time of grief, but I will see you again and you will rejoice, and no one will take away your joy. John 16:20,22

November 13, 2012, 10:01 p.m.

Hey Sweetie,

Crawling into our bed again without you. I've missed you so much. I had some good memories of you today and that helped me cope. I smile when I think of how you used to dance with me in the kitchen because you liked a song playing on the radio.

I'm still waiting for your cause of death. I don't know how God took you home. I am certain it was peaceful and for that I am thankful. He knew how much you suffered on earth, so in death, He did not allow you to suffer.

I wish I could have told you goodbye, Sweetie—told you how much I loved you and how thankful I was for the sacrifices you made for me. I couldn't have asked for a better guy. You loved me like no other—how lucky for me!

November 17, 2012, 2:47 a.m.

Tough day today, Sweetie. The tears fall often and don't seem to stop. Everything is so empty. I think about our dreams, our future travel plans, our hopes, our love for each other and my heart just aches.

November 21, 2012, 2:31 a.m.

Oh, Sweetie. My sleep is so broken. I wake often and expect you'll be by my side, but you're not. I don't know how long it will take before sleep will be normal once again. Everyone says it will take time—no one is sure how much time. I miss you.

November 25, 2012, 10:42 p.m.

I miss you every day and every night. This emptiness doesn't feel like it will ever go away. Nothing fills my heart like you did. I love you.

November 26, 2012, 5:56 a.m.

Waking up without you again, Sweetie. I still don't know why you aren't with me. The room is chilly and if you were here, I'd put the coffee on and come back to bed to snuggle with you until it was done. Then you could get up and bring us a cup.

I am sad without you.

The Strength of Sampson

Sitting alone in the coffee shop normally wouldn't bother me, but things were different now. The choice to be alone hadn't been mine. Removing the lid from the Styrofoam cup, I used a black plastic stick to stir in some cream. I imagined Willie's methodical movements as he stirred my coffee with a silver spoon, clanking it into a ceramic cup. Oh, how I missed him! Lonely, lonely days.

Scents of hazelnut and French vanilla blended with the aroma of roasted coffee beans. Leaning back in the chair, I looked around. A framed picture of a steaming coffee cup on an olive green wall. Round, wooden tables with iron legs and matching chairs. Floor to ceiling windows to my left providing an ample view of the snow outside. A bronze-colored terrazzo floor. Everything appeared the same, but I knew it all had changed.

Brushing my hair back over my ears, the emptiness swept over me and through me. My hair had been a strong connection to Willie. I allowed my hand to linger on the back of my head. What I wouldn't give to see his twinkling eyes and his mischievous grin, to have him here to share a cup of coffee with me.

I held the cup between my hands to savor the warmth.

Even though I had gladly given Willie my hair, a sadness filled me and I experienced a void whenever I brushed, washed, or dried what little I had left. With Willie, my blond locks hung halfway down my back. Now, my style was chin length.

Running my fingers through my hair again, I acknowledged this shorter style was indeed a godsend. Much easier to care for, and these days I didn't care for much.

Perhaps I am like Sampson and my strength, reliant on my hair, would return as my hair grew longer. I quickly vetoed that idea. When I had long hair, I had my husband, the source of my strength. Tears stung my eyes.

I picked up the cup of coffee and took a small sip. As I set it back down on the table, I caught sight of the San Damiano cross that hung on the wall. On the cross, the death, resurrection, and ascension of Christ had been depicted in pictures in bold reds, golds, blues, and greens. The central figure, Jesus Christ, his bright white body in full stature, a halo surrounding his head, tendered light, hope. What a deep contrast to the smaller characters and the darker colors on the rest of the cross. Jesus held his arms wide open, and at that moment I knew my strength did not come from my hair or my husband. It came from Jesus Christ, my Savior.

> *When Jesus spoke again to the people, he said, "I am the light of the world. Whoever follows me will never walk in darkness, but will have the light of life."*
> *John 8:12*

November 27, 2012, 10:29 p.m.

I miss the TV blaring and the loud music. Funny how you think you only want peace and quiet and then you get it and find out, it is not what you wanted at all.

November 30, 2012, 9:32 p.m.

Tough times for me today. Two calls from the funeral home. One to say that your laminated obituaries were ready and one to say it no longer said "pending" on your death certificate. Now I will know why you are gone—the thought brings me no relief.

Will I ever get over you, Sweetie? Will I ever stop missing you? Will my heart ever, ever stop aching? Oh, how I wish you were home with me!

December 3, 2012, 11:08 p.m.

Hey, Sweetie. I am a little puzzled tonight. I picked up your death certificate and the cause of death is ""Fentanyl Toxicity." The doctor's office tested your levels on October 5th. I am so confused right now.

December 4, 2012, 11:14 p.m.

Made it through another day my dear. How, I'll never know. Gosh, how I miss having you here with me! I looked up Fentanyl Toxicity on the computer. Kicking myself now—why didn't I see the signs—the memory problems, the balance, the sleep, the mood swings? I blamed it all on your stroke and you were dying before my eyes. It makes me so sad.

And angry! The very people who were supposed to care for you, killed you. You didn't want to use that damn medication and they didn't care.

December 8, 2012, 10:11 p.m.

Rough day today—trying to get excited about Christmas and it makes me miss you all the more! Everyone tells me you would want me to be happy; they just don't tell me how to do that without you.

I cried lots of tears today—they just fall uncontrollably at random times.

Why couldn't I save you, Sweetie? Why couldn't I have you here with me? It is so hard to find joy—in anything. All the things we did together, the interests we shared, the simple, everyday things like drinking coffee and doing the crossword puzzle—none of it is the same.

Will life ever feel good again?

Chapter 9

Artificial Christmas

"Here you go, Mom," Bud said as he came up the basement stairs holding an eight-foot balsam pine covered in a tree disposal bag. "Where are we going to put this?"

"Where we always do," I answered. Bud's allergies ceased our yearly hunt for the perfect Christmas tree. An artificial tree stored downstairs, decorated with lights and garland, substituted for the real thing for many years now.

"But what about . . . What did you do with Dad's urn?"

"Moved it to the bedroom. Didn't really think we wanted it by the tree," I said. The urn had sat in the same spot since Jeane had brought Willie home. A red rose laid over the top of it by Jasmine had long since dried and lost its sweet scent. I moved that, too.

Bud placed the tree in the corner and pulled the white plastic bag off of it. "Is that all you need, Mom?"

"You don't want to help me put the ornaments on it?" I asked. Willie had a sweet tooth, so the glass ornaments this year resembled candy bars—M&M's, Reese's, Almond Joy, Mounds, Twizzlers, Nestle's miniatures—all his favorites.

"Not really my thing, Mom," Bud said as he gave me a little hug.

"Love you." He disappeared around the corner and up the stairs, leaving me alone with the ghosts of Christmas past.

As I manipulated the branches so they resembled a real tree, I located the electrical cords for the blue lights and the yellow star. Blue lights. How appropriate. I plugged in the cord, resulting in a half-lit tree and no glow from the star. After repositioning the light strands, I made another attempt with the same results.

Why can't anything be easy?

I pulled the plug from the socket and laid down on the black leather sofa. Time for some music. "Blue Christmas" sung by Elvis Presley. "It Won't be Christmas Without You" sung by Brooks & Dunn. "All I Want for Christmas is You" sung by Vince Vance and the Valiants.

Perhaps, I should just take a cruise. Go somewhere far away, sleep the day away, and the whole world would disappear. I looked at the barren and dark green tree.

Lifeless. Just like me.

* * *

As I removed my boots in the back entryway, I had mixed emotions when hearing voices inside the house. *What is it now?*

As I opened the door, I heard Rachael's cheerful greeting. "Hey, Mom. Bud said you had trouble with the lights on the tree so we fixed them for you."

Tears of joy stung my eyes. "Thank you. And, you put an angel on the top," I said.

"Yeah. Just one I had at home. We couldn't get the star to work. Besides, I thought you'd prefer an angel this year," Rachael said as she hugged me. "I love you, Mama." She carefully unfolded white tissue paper and began hanging ornaments on the tree.

"You know Dad wouldn't like these, don't you?" she asked, holding up one of the candy bar ornaments.

I raised my eyebrows. "Because you can't eat them?" She nodded her head and we both laughed.

"Maybe instead of hanging candy canes on the tree this year, we should hang Tootsie Pops," Rachael suggested. "Dad loved them."

"That he did. I am still finding the sticks! I do have an extra bag in the bedroom. I bought them to put in the Quaker Oats cookie jars. I want the girls to have those, because they always knew that's where Grandpa kept the Tootsie Pops."

"How are you going to do that with one cookie jar, Mom?"

"I actually have two of them. You know your Dad. It never hurts to have a spare," I answered.

Together we laughed, reminisced, and decorated the tree. Rachael put on some music. "Have a Holly Jolly Christmas" sung by Burl Ives. "Walking in a Winter Wonderland" sung by Perry Como. "Jingle Bell Rock" sung by Bobby Helms.

Upbeat. Uplifting. Optimistic.

Perhaps running away didn't need to be an option.

The cedars in the garden of God could not rival it, nor could the pine trees equal its boughs, nor could the plane trees compare with its branches – no tree in the garden of God could match its beauty. Ezekiel 31:8

December 13, 2012, 10:26 p.m.

Hello, Sweetie. Are you dancing tonight? Are you inspecting the welds on the pearly gates? Whatever you are doing, I know it is pain-free.

I went and talked to a counselor today and it really helped to have someone objective to talk to. I feel a sense of relief tonight and I am counting all the blessings we shared.

I miss you, Sweetie. I need you to laugh with, to hug, to kiss, to snuggle with, to give me a reason to make coffee in the morning. You know I still need you.

December 17, 2012, 10:12 p.m.

I can't seem to get myself motivated these days. My whole routine is out of whack without you here. I don't make coffee or read the paper or stay on my own side of the bed. Tears still fall and there is no one to hold me close and tell me it will be okay. Of course, if I had that, I wouldn't have the tears, would I?

December 18, 2012, 5:21 a.m.

Woke up this morning to thoughts of our last evening together. Why didn't I realize the angel of death was knocking on the door? Oh, Sweetie, why, why, why do I have to be without you? I know in spirit you are with me. I know I shall always have our memories. No one can rob me of those, but my days are so long without you by my side. I physically can't reach out and touch you—I only have your pillow to hug. It is the closest thing to you.

I close my eyes and I can bring you back to me—your smile, your laugh, your twinkling eyes. You were my Santa Claus.

But it all doesn't really bring you back to me. It doesn't make the hurt any less.

Cross My Heart

The delicate gold chain slipped through my fingers, but I held tight to the gold cross. I rubbed it between my thumb and my index finger to feel the texture created by the ornate pattern of swirls and curly cues.

"Guess you win, Sweetie," I said before hooking the chain at the back of my neck, allowing the cross to hang to the cleavage of my breasts. I held my hand over it then, recalling the day I received it.

Christmas 2011. Willie and I held our usual seats on the left end of the sofa, he dressed in his blue and green plaid flannel robe and I in my pink one. Neither matched the red and white Santa hats on our heads.

Bud, our Santa, said, "This one is for you, Mom." He handed me a tiny box wrapped in a silver hound's tooth pattern and topped with a vibrant purple curly ribbon. I smiled at Willie as I reached for it. The ornate paper and festive bow let me know it came from him. He had always been all thumbs when it came to wrapping, so he'd paid extra for that.

"I know. It's probably stupid," he said. "Maybe next year I'll do something different."

"No, Sweetie," I responded. "I love my crosses."

"But you always know what it is," he said.

"Not exactly. You always surprise me." I couldn't remember a Christmas he hadn't bought me a cross. Though all tiny and delicate, none were the same—one adorned with my birthstone, one with a diamond in the center of polished silver, one a textured gold with onyx. As I unwrapped this one, the larger size caught me unaware. An open design reminiscent of antique jewelry, it provided the feminine touch I so adored.

"It's a little different," he said. "If you don't like it, you can always take it back."

After hooking the necklace around my neck, I gave him a kiss. "Nonsense," I said. "I love it and I love getting my crosses. Don't change that."

The feel of the cross between my thumb and index finger brought me back to the present.

"Bud, are you ready to go Christmas shopping?" I hollered up the stairs.

***

"What are we doing here?" Bud asked.

People moved about under the fluorescent lights in the departments around us and I could make out the lively sounds of Christmas carols playing. I relished being the only customer at the jewelry counter.

"Your dad always got me a cross," I said, "so I am getting my cross." Bud raised his eyebrows slightly, but he didn't say a word.

Rows of crosses in precious metals, all shapes and sizes, filled the glass cases. Some were adorned with engraved patterns, others with gems, and others' beauty came from their simplicity. The lights in the case reflected off them like the stars in the heavens.

"Can I help you?" the salesclerk asked.

"I'd like that cross right there," I said, pointing out a gold one with a red stone heart in the center.

"Shall I gift wrap it?" the clerk asked as she reached for the cross. Bud's eyebrows raised higher and he shook his head.

I smiled at him and laughed. "No, that's not necessary." I had the cross and that alone would bring my sweetie back to me.

And over all these virtues put on love, which binds them all together in perfect unity. Colossians 3:14

December 21, 2012, 10:28 p.m.

I'm still missing you, darling, but I am taking Jasmine's advice and bringing home a cat tomorrow. It won't be you, but it will be company. I do not like being alone.

Company. Comfort. Cat.

"Fine. We can go look, but I am not getting a cat right now. I can barely take care of myself," I said as I pulled on my purple wool coat and wrapped the silver scarf around my neck.

Bud, Jasmine, and I piled into the van and headed to the Bay Area Humane Society. My family had been pushing me to adopt a cat to keep me company. None of them seemed to understand how hard it was just getting out of bed every day.

"Are you coming?" Bud held the door to the humane society open and Jasmine bounced up and down just inside. If only I had half their enthusiasm. With much effort, I hopped out of the van and joined them.

Inside, the smell of pet food and bleach greeted us. To the left, a glass door led into the area where the cats roamed. Jasmine practically pushed me in there. Cats climbed and played everywhere. White ones, black ones, gray ones, orange ones, and many in color combinations. Big cats, small cats, and in-between cats. Playful cats. Lazy cats. Curious cats.

And I had no interest in any of them.

"Oh, Grandma," Jasmine said. "Look at her." She held a tiny, cream-colored cat that purred contently as Jasmine rubbed her neck.

"Hey, Ma. Here's a calico. You always said if you got another cat, you wanted a calico," Bud said, petting a large orange, black, and white cat as it sprawled out on a carpeted shelf, meowing loudly.

"It's too noisy," I said. I pulled my purse close, forming a barrier between me and the furry creatures all around me. I watched as my granddaughter eagerly played. I watched as my son searched for the perfect cat for his mother. I watched as a small black and white tuxedo cat ignored the invitations to wrestle from her peers. She turned her nose upward, choosing to look off in the distance rather than meet their gaze head on. She approached my granddaughter and promptly laid down and began her bathing ritual.

"I like this one," I said, pointing her out. The kids wasted no time in contacting the staff so we could visit the tiny cat in a private room. Bud carried her in, cradling her like a baby and scratching her belly. Jasmine took her next and I listened to her rhythmic purr as she sat in Jasmine's lap, craning her neck back, begging to have it rubbed more and more.

I recalled sitting with Jasmine on the back stoop two years prior. She had been eight years old and her great-grandfather had passed away. We found comfort sitting quietly with one another as we mourned that deep loss.

"Grams, what would you do if something happened to Gramps?" she asked.

"I don't know, honey. I just don't know."

She returned to her sitting posture, knees bent toward her chest, elbows resting on her knees and supporting her head in her hands. Her light brown hair fell over her shoulders and down her back. My heart broke to see her perfect world shattered. We stared out at a snow-covered landscape. Emptiness.

Suddenly she spoke. "You could get a cat."

I hugged her. "You think so?" I asked as I laughed.

My thoughts were interrupted by the face of a black and white cat coming toward me. "Here, Grams. You hold her now. She's so sweet," Jasmine said.

I relinquished my purse and took the furry little ball. "What's wrong with her eye?" I asked.

"They said as far as they know, she's a stray. She has scar tissue on her eye from fighting with another cat," Bud said. Holding her, I could tell she barely weighed nine pounds if even that. I shuddered to think of another cat bullying her and hugged her closer, before handing her back to Jasmine so I could go fill out the adoption paperwork. This little cat and I both needed someone to love.

Three days passed before she had a name. "Hey, Ma. I figured out a name for her. Tootsie," Bud said. The name had not been inspired by her four white paws.

"That's perfect!" Willie loved Tootsie Pops, and now I would love Tootsie. Little did I know how getting a cat would bring so much comfort.

I will turn their mourning into gladness; I will give them comfort and joy instead of sorrow.
Jeremiah 31:13b.

December 23, 2012, 9:52 p.m.

Christmas Eve is tomorrow—my first one without you. Everyone tells me all the first will be the toughest, but I will confess to you that I've spent over two months going to bed alone and waking up alone and it is not getting any easier.

I don't cry as often, but it doesn't mean it hurts any less. Such a lonely, lonely world when the one you love is gone.

It Won't Be Christmas Without You

As I wrapped my hands around the pew seat and shrugged my shoulders, I contemplated the hereafter. This is how Christmas Eve always started—a late-afternoon church service. I straightened one of the red tiers on my dress, running my hand over it gently, firmly; feeling in control . . . of something.

After church, the kids and grandkids would head over to the house for a family meal. Our patriarch would be missing. I had debated about setting his place for someone else or leaving it unoccupied to resemble the emptiness we all felt. In the end, I set the place.

Traditionally, dinner had been followed by Willie "not feeling well" and needing to lie down while the rest of the family ventured out to look at Christmas lights. While we drove around oooing and aaahing over the holiday displays and Willie "slept," Santa visited, placing gifts beneath the tree for little ones to discover upon our return. I smiled as I recalled the excitement—feet stomping up and down, hands clapping, and eyes wide.

"Santa came! Santa came!" Delightful giggles accompanied it all.

"Then you'd better go get Grandpa up so we can open gifts," I'd say.

93

Gifts. Always the cross in its professionally wrapped jewelry box. This year it would be no surprise. I'd purchased it myself. And then a present that would render me speechless. Something that I wouldn't buy for myself or even realize I needed or wanted. That I would miss. Him I would miss.

Jasmine nudged me. Church had ended. Time to head home.

Christmas Eve service failed to fill my heart in the usual way and the Christmas light tour had been vetoed. We'd have dinner and open the gifts already delivered by my co-workers from St. Mary's Hospital Medical Center Rehab Services.

We ate from festive Christmas paper plates and used matching paper napkins. Pink Moscato wine filled the cobalt-blue stemmed glasses, a change from the years of sparkling grape juice. Willie, a recovered alcoholic, celebrated twenty-three years of sobriety the day before he joined his Lord and Savior.

Once we finished eating, we gathered around the slender Christmas tree decorated with blue lights, replica candy bar ornaments, real Tootsie Pops, and a white and gold-clad angel.

Bud, traditionally the one to pass out gifts, settled in next to the tree. Some things stayed the same.

The kids laughed and joked as they opened their gifts. I prayed Willie could see them.

"Bud, will you give Lexi and Jasmine those boxes wrapped in the blue angel paper with the silver bows?" I asked. "I want them to open them together."

The granddaughters unwrapped the packages, each lifting out a tissue paper-wrapped red, white, and blue Quaker Oats ceramic cookie jar.

Lexi looked at me, disbelief on her face. "Grandma, where did you get these?"

"Grandpa bought them," I said. "I filled them with Tootsie Pops for you, just like he did."

"Grandpa bought both of them?" Lexi asked.

"Yes, he did."

She held her cookie jar close. "That makes it even more special."

"Hey, Mom. This one is for you," Bud said. I reached out and took the festively wrapped package with the gold and white cloth bow. About the size of a medium book, I could handle it easily.

"That's a Kindle," Rachael said.

"No, it's not," I said. "I never said I wanted a Kindle."

"Yes, it is. I recognize the box," Rachael said.

I opened the gift, confirming her suspicions. A Kindle. A perfect something I had not realized I wanted or needed. Unknowingly, my co-workers had delivered a part of Willie home to me. I felt the presence of God as He continued to bless me, in spite of my loss.

> *Every good and perfect gift is from above, coming down from the Father of the heavenly lights, who does not change like shifting shadows. James 1:17*

December 25, 2012, 10:24 p.m.

I woke up sad today. I had Christmas with the kids yesterday, but I usually spent Christmas Day with you. I took the tree down. I am ready for Christmas to be over. I've always loved the beauty of the tree, but this year, it just makes me sad.

When does it get easier to be without the love of your life? When does it seem like you want to get out of bed or face the day?

Chapter 10

The "W" Word

The arctic wind sweeping around the corner of the house greeted me and challenged my balancing skills as I struggled to get the back door unlocked. Even a key in a lock didn't seem to want to work in these frigid temperatures. Finally inside, I quickly slammed the door shut. Stomping my feet removed the snow before I kicked off my boots in the back entryway.

I stopped and listened.

Silence.

No sound of his footsteps coming to greet me. No sound of coffee brewing. No sound of the television or radio playing. The absence of all those sounds reminded me how much I missed my husband. Coming home to an empty house had not been on my bucket list.

Three steps up from the back entry way took me into the kitchen, where I placed my bags on the table before going to hang up my coat. I ran my gloved hand over the oak tabletop, another flea market find that he had refinished. Memories everywhere.

Once the deep purple coat and silver scarf had been shed, I reached for my pastel pink bathrobe and threw it on right over my clothes. No one to keep me warm on a cold winter day. Did anyone really understand what it meant to lose your husband? How many times had I said, "I'm sorry" to someone who lost their spouse? I wrapped my arms around myself. Clearly, I didn't understand before, but now I walked that path.

I sighed deeply as I plopped down in the pressback kitchen chair. What would I do with another long, lonely night? I caught a glimpse of one of the items I had sat on the table, a Christmas gift bag my friend, Susan, had dropped off for me in the afternoon. Adorned with an angel and silver ribbon, it looked festive, inviting, and comforting.

I pulled out the green tissue paper that had been tucked inside to hide the contents. Inside, I found a miniature snowman cookie jar containing shortbread cookies and a Russell Stover box of chocolates. Willie would love that. He did have a thing for sweets. Tucked along the side of the bag I discovered a book on grief. It had been written by a woman who lost her husband. At last, someone that understood.

With a cup of hot lemon tea and my new book, I headed in to curl up on the couch and seek reassurance. The quilt I had made from T-shirts the family had once treasured lay there, and I pulled it up over my legs to help keep me warm. I started to read while I sipped at the tea. I felt comforted in knowing this would be just what I needed.

Only a few pages in, I flung the book aside. With the quilt tossed from my lap, I stood abruptly. Grabbing the tea, I took another sip and paced across the braided rug. *Had I really just read that?* The word had not touched my lips. It couldn't even be thought about and yet right there, in black and white, it had been written and her husband wasn't even dead yet. I shed the bathrobe as I walked back and forth.

My husband passed away. I lost my husband. Willie is no longer with me. My husband is gone. I bet I could list "Twenty ways to say your husband is in heaven and you're the 'W' word" without using "dead" or the "W" word. How could that author even think of that word before her husband had gone?

My pacing slowed and my heartbeat returned to near normal. She did have time to plan for that part, though. I did not. Thrust upon me one unsuspecting morning left me no time for preparation. One day I was a wife and the next I was not. Still marching through the living room, I resolved not to open that book again.

Unable to resist the temptation, I did pick up the devotional book again. Within its covers, I discovered that even women who have lost their husbands can survive, even if they can't say the "W" word.

> *The king asked her, "What is troubling you?" She said,*
> *"I am indeed a widow; my husband is dead."*
> *2 Samuel 14:5*

December 31, 2012, 11:16 p.m.

I walked on the treadmill, trying to pound the life back into you. I still need you, yet that is impossible. It was time for your worldly pain to end. It was God's plan, not ours. I know I was not prepared, but God prepared a place for you.

I know not what God has planned for me. I know not what this experience will prepare me for, but in time, I know God will open my eyes and I will understand. That does not make it any easier.

I pray, Sweetie. I pray for strength. Strength to face the day. Strength to get through the day. Strength to be without my sweetie.

January 5, 2013, 6:25 a.m.

I still wake expecting you to be here. You'd do that little reassuring laugh of yours when I'd tell you about this nightmare I've been having and you'd say, "You can't get rid of me that easily."

January 9, 2013, 10:13 p.m.

I have to renew my CPR for work. It is going to be tough. It only makes me think of you. I'll have to pray for more strength because that is the only way I'll get through it—if I even get through it. It is heavy on my mind.

January 17, 2013, 9:41 p.m.
Saw the doctor today and I won't be joining you any time soon. I don't really know if that should be a happy or a sad face.

January 20, 2013, 5:50 a.m.
Good morning, Sweetie. Down in the dumps this morning. I can't seem to get all the signs of fentanyl toxicity out of my mind. It seems so senseless that you're gone when all the signs were there. Why didn't they acknowledge that? I know I must stop dwelling on it, but it is so hard when every day I wake up, you are not here. Is this the angry stage I am supposed to go through?

January 21, 2013, 10:26 p.m.
Watching some home movies tonight so I can see you again. Told the kids I am just cleaning some things up, but I really want to see your smile, hear your laugh, listen to your voice.

Interlacing Hope Amidst Despair

I pulled the soiled cuffs of Willie's tan, maroon, and gray plaid flannel shirt over my hands and tightened the strings of the gray sweatshirt hood. Class hadn't started and I already prayed for the eight warm bodies to heat up the garage turned workshop at Swanstone Gardens. *Why hadn't I told Michelle I had plans today? That I'd be too busy to take a class? I could still be home, cozy in my bed.*

"Everyone take the packet of reeds that is clipped together in front of them. Lay them out on the table, alternating long and short," Janet said.

Skeptical, I picked up the packet of reeds, unsure that the clipped bundle would turn into a basket with my two hands. Regardless, I laid out the reeds, carefully arranging them according to the pencil marks Janet had put there prior to class.

"How did you do, Mama?" Rachael asked.

I laid the weighted bar across the strips to hold them in place. "Just not sure this is going to be a basket," I said.

Michelle laughed. "It's a good thing we have Rising Ray to help us." I smiled. Michelle had positive nicknames for everyone, even me. Divine Deb. Only I did not feel so divine today.

Janet continued with her instruction and soon we all had the basket base weaved. "Wow, Deb. That's foundational," Michelle said, laughing again. Her optimistic spirit was good for me.

"Next, we'll upset the reeds," Janet said as she demonstrated the technique, her skill as an artisan clearly evident.

We began upsetting the reeds on our own bases, clothes pinning them together at the corners. In the midst of all the thrashing, I could sense that this might actually be a basket. For the first time today, I felt at peace delving into unknown territory, enjoying something I hadn't done and living through it. I glanced at my daughter and my friends, Michelle and Susan, and said a silent prayer of thanks to have friends who would give up their Saturday to help me heal.

Together, we weaved the reeds of our own baskets. Though similar shapes, it became evident that some of us wove tighter than others. Rachael showed up with the awl and helped me align things when I lost direction. Soon our baskets developed their own personalities as we chose dyed reeds and sweetgrass braids to incorporate.

We worked up until lunch and then into the early evening hours to complete our baskets. I felt accomplished. I had made a basket. I hadn't spent the day hibernating in my room or in the recliner or crying.

This basket stood for something. Survival. It hadn't come easy, but in the end, success was mine and in that, I saw hope.

> *Guide me in your truth and teach me, for you are God*
> *my Savior, and my hope is in you all day long.*
> *Psalm 25:5*

January 29, 2013, 2:47 a.m.

Middle of the night darling and I am thinking about you. I met with an attorney yesterday about a possible medical lawsuit because of the fentanyl that killed you. The fentanyl that did you in. The fentanyl that you begged to be taken off of. Like your medical history, it is all so complicated.

I just don't know, darling. They dangle money in front of me. What would you say you're worth?

I don't want another spouse to go through what I am. I want the doctors to actually pay attention to what they are giving patients and to really heed the signs of toxicity. None of that can be guaranteed.

There must be another way.

I may just have to write them a letter to have my say. It's all so complicated.

I love you and I miss you.

Second Chances

"Waves of Arctic air are expected to continue to sweep into the area today with an expected high of three below," the weatherman announced.

I pulled the green and gold fleece blanket up tighter around my shoulders, adjusted the yellow throw pillow under my head, and turned in the recliner so I had a view out the living room window. Everything covered in white, stark and desolate. Wind whipped around the house as though even it sought refuge from the bitter temperatures. Normally, I didn't mind winter and its cold temperatures, because I had a warm body to curl up with.

"Lord, why does it have to be so cold this year?"

"With the dangerously low temperatures, authorities are urging the homeless to seek shelter. On Monday morning, a thirty-eight-year-old man found dead outside his home most likely died from hypothermia and cold exposure."

I slid my hand out from under the blanket long enough to turn off the television with the remote. The news had done nothing to cheer me up.

As I sat there, I attempted to focus on my loneliness, but my thoughts only centered on how different today would be if Willie lie beside me. The aroma of steaming hot coffee would fill the air, a contrast to the bitter cold. A warm arm covered in blue and green flannel would rest around my shoulders and I'd feel a gentle pull in his direction.

"You warm enough, darling? I can't have my Sweetie getting cold." I closed my eyes, imaging the soft kiss he'd place on top of my head.

"I miss you, Sweetie. Oh, how I miss you."

I felt lifeless as I continued to lie in the chair. Thoughts of the sacrifices Willie had made for me and others fleeted in and out of my mind. Sometimes I hadn't understood.

"I can't believe you gave him money. You know what his track record is!" I'd said once.

"Darling, everyone deserves a second chance," he replied, giving me a squeeze. I prayed he knew what he was doing.

Willie had helped many others, probably because we experienced rough times ourselves. I suppose he never forgot that. I pulled the throw even tighter around me. Why couldn't I get warm inside my own house?

I thought about the homeless who had no house. I thought about Willie's winter clothing, assembled neatly in his dresser drawers. Unused when others suffered from hypothermia.

Everyone deserves a second chance, darling.

Reaching for the laptop computer, I did a search for "St. John's Homeless Shelter." Two clicks later, their wish list displayed on my computer. The list included thermal underwear, flannel shirts, reading glasses, ear plugs, winter outerwear, and men's jeans.

Willie could continue helping others. I tossed the fleece blanket aside and headed to the bedroom. I unpacked his drawers, piling navy blue thermal underwear and denim jeans high on the bed, and added to the stack from a basket he'd kept in the bottom of the closet. After throwing on his winter coats, insulated coveralls, and six flannel shirts still wrapped in plastic, the bed disappeared.

In the top drawer, I pulled out a Ziploc bag full of ear plugs and another bag that concealed its contents in white tissue paper. The tissue paper rustled softly as I unwrapped it, and when I saw the contents, I laughed out loud. Reading glasses. Lots and lots of reading glasses. I shook my head and I could hear his voice. "What? They're cheap, darling, and it doesn't hurt to have an extra pair around."

While getting plastic bags from the kitchen to transport everything, I spotted more glasses in the wooden cheese box that sat on the table. I found more on the desk in our home office. As I packed things into the bags, I noticed the nightstand drawer next to his side of the bed. Sure enough, more glasses. I counted them as I placed them in a shoe box.

After donning my winter coat, I took my husband's things and put them in the back of the van and headed straight to the shelter. When I arrived, I stood shivering in the cold as no one had yet answered the buzzer. I pushed it again and just before I planned to leave, I saw two bodies heading in my direction.

"Can I help you?" the female said.

"I have some things to donate to the shelter," I said. "They were my husband's things. He doesn't need them anymore. I lost him in October." Hard as I tried, I could not control the tears.

The woman grabbed my gloved hands. "I'm so sorry for your loss."

"Let me help you get the rest," a man said, placing a hand on my shoulder. Together, we brought in the remaining items.

"He was a welder and worked outside a lot, so he had plenty of long underwear. He had brand new flannel shirts he was saving until the others wore out. And this . . . this is over thirty pairs of reading glasses." I managed to laugh. "He may have been a little obsessive."

As I drove away from the shelter, I prayed. "Thank you, God. Today, my husband helped thirty-three people to see."

And we know that in all things God works for the good of those who love him, who have been called according to his purpose. Romans 8:28

January 31, 2013, 5:14 a.m.

I wake in the night and even though the temperatures are fine, I am cold. I am without you. I wake in the morning and even though silence lurks, I search for your voice. I am without you. I wake in the night and even though I am alone, I reach out for you. Finally, reality sets in. You are not here. You have moved on to heaven.

January 31, 2013, 10:09 p.m.

Going to bed, Sweetie, but I wanted to tell you that Jasmine is writing a biography for school. She had to write on someone interesting and that someone is you! She misses you, too.

February 2, 2013, 6:33 a.m.

The nights are long; the days are long. I need to busy my mind to keep from hurting so much, but it is not getting any easier. The days are empty. I will try to make it a productive Saturday. I will try to avoid wasting the day, but I will need strength, much strength.

February 4, 2013, 9:21 p.m.

Kind of a depressing day. I didn't even get dressed until after noon. Some days are so long. I just want to drop out of life for a while. I know you want me to be happy. I just have not found a way to do that yet. Happiness and you went hand in hand. Hope you can pray for me from heaven because I need the strength.

February 7, 2013, 5:36 a.m.

It's probably silly, but when I was cleaning out your drawer the other day, I found some of your partially used ChapSticks and now I am using them. It feels like I can have your lips on mine once again! Not exactly the same, but as close as I can get right now.

Blessings in Disguise

I considered going back home even as I pulled into the parking lot and turned off the ignition. I picked up the postcard from the passenger seat. GriefShare. Perhaps another time would be better, but I felt God nudging me. I pulled the silver vinyl strap of my purse over my right shoulder, tightened the purple wool collar of my coat around my neck, and opened the van door. The February winds ushered me into the building.

Inside the very funeral home that laid my husband to rest, I found the meeting room. Rows of tables and chairs had been set up to face a television screen. A continental breakfast of juices, sweet rolls, and coffee awaited attendees in the same area where Willie had laid in his casket, awaiting my final approval for his going away. I avoided the breakfast spread and chose a seat on the opposite side of the room, away from any other attendees. I did not feel very social.

The war went on in my mind. Perhaps, it would be best to try this another time. I started to rise. "Good morning," a rather heavy-set man said. His short red hair stuck up from the back of his head and his smile revealed less than perfect teeth. "My name's Curtis. We do have breakfast set up, if you'd like something. I'd like to welcome you this morning and let you know we'll get started shortly." I sat back down.

Before long, Curtis introduced himself and the other speakers to the group. After watching a brief video, they passed out blank sheets of paper.

"Everyone fold your paper in half the long way," Curtis instructed, demonstrating as he walked back and forth. "Okay, open it back up. At the top of the paper, across the folded line, write down the year you were born and on the bottom of it write down this year. Don't worry. No one else will see these unless you want them to. Now, on the left side of the paper, I want you to list the losses you've experienced in your life."

This is supposed to help me? Looking at sad times in my life? Doesn't he realize I am grieving? I shook my head and wrote on the sheet, including "the loss of a healthy child." I stared into space and thought.

Once both of our daughters attended school all day and all baby items had been dispersed to others in need, God blessed us with another child. When I held that eight-pound boy in my arms the first time, I wondered what God was thinking. It had been a long time since I cared for a newborn and I felt totally unequipped to be his mother. Still, God had entrusted the care of this little guy to me.

We brought Bud home from the hospital with a large scab where the tip of his nose should have been. Most of his body had some type of rash, supposedly a heat rash. Turns out my little man had allergies to something in the hospital linens.

Bud spent the first year of his life making frequent doctor visits. Not the usual well-baby checks, rather the something's wrong kind of visits. He struggled to breathe as his little nose, whose scab finally healed, filled with mucus. At times, he worked so hard to breathe that the area between his belly and his back flattened like a tortilla shell. Or he coughed and coughed and coughed. I begged and pleaded with God to help me with my son. I had never had a sick child and I really had no idea how to care for one.

Unbeknownst to me, God answered my prayers in an unexpected way—by moving me over three hours from all my family and friends in South Beloit, Illinois. Willie took a supervisor position at a recycling center in Green Bay, Wisconsin, a city of approximately 100,000 strangers. In one month, his health insurance would kick in and I could find a pediatrician for our son.

At the end of our first week in Green Bay, I sat on the stoop next to the telephone book opened to "physicians." My rasping, gasping baby lay on my legs, his head at my knees. I had never seen someone put that much exertion into breathing. Finding a doctor couldn't wait.

Starting at the beginning of the alphabet, I began calling pediatricians.

"Hello. My son needs to see a doctor. He is having trouble breathing," I said into the phone.

"Who's his doctor, please?"

"We just moved to the area. He doesn't have one yet," I responded.

"We're not taking new patients, if they are sick. You'll have to take him to the emergency room."

The same conversation repeated over and over. Nearing the end of the listings didn't deter me. We could not afford an emergency department bill and Bud needed to see a doctor. With tears streaming down my cheeks, the numbers became difficult to see, but with God's help, I managed to dial the West Side Clinic.

The doctor on call agreed to see my son. Three hours after we entered her office, after she had thoroughly examined him and given him a nebulizer treatment, she asked, "How long has he had asthma?" No one had ever used that word in connection with my son. My world came crashing down.

Bud did not go home from the doctor's office. He went straight to the hospital, where he stayed for ten days. When the doctor's bill came, a red stamp marked the top of the bill. It said, "No charge." When we recite the Lord's Prayer, we say "Give us this day our daily bread," and that is exactly what the Lord did.

Over the next several years, we learned how to care for a child with asthma. We learned about medicines, positioning, triggers, and breathing techniques. We learned what to do in an emergency, when to call the doctor, and when to head to the hospital's emergency room. He was definitely not a healthy child.

Curtis's voice brought me back to the present. "Now on the right side of your paper, write down the blessings you have had in life."

Ah. An activity that would actually be comforting for a grieving woman.

I began writing. Soon I noticed a pattern and felt comforted in my soul. I wrote down "Being able to ease the fear in patients with breathing problems." Many of the losses I had experienced turned to blessings later on the timeline.

God uses everything for his own good, something I am well aware of, but for the first time it really hit home for me. This hurting, this feeling lost did not leave me alone; it drew me closer to God and somehow, someday, this experience would shape me into who God wants me to be.

He has made everything beautiful in its time.
Ecclesiastes 3:11a

February 9, 2013, 10:16 p.m.

It's been an emotionally draining day. I attended a seminar on dealing with grief and loss. I am not over you by any means. The tears flowed and flowed, but I am happy to report I am perfectly normal. I grieve not only the physical loss of your being, but also the loss of our dreams, our hopes, and plans for the future, and it's all okay. I don't know when it will get better, but I know someday it will.

February 13, 2013, 10:17 p.m.

Ash Wednesday, Sweetie. I went to church tonight. Clung to my cross and wore the scarf I bought to wear for your service. It all makes me feel like I've got you with me. I know you are in my heart, too. You always said you couldn't live without me, but now I've got to figure out how to live without you. I draw on strength through our memories together and the stories I tell. I love you, darling. You know I do.

February 15, 2013, 9:54 p.m.

Hey, Sweetie. I watched the DVD from your service yesterday before I went to sleep—my way of having you with me on Valentine's Day. We had a lot of good memories—I'll always be thankful for that.

February 16, 2013, 5:06 a.m.

Good morning, Sweetie. I write that and I can see your smile—you must have slept well. I put your pillow along my back last night and leaned into it so I could feel like you were in bed with me.

You know my routine has changed in the mornings. After I wash my face, I put under-eye concealer on to hide the dark circles and lipstick to draw attention away from my sad eyes. I am sleeping better, but still not enough. I think this long, cold winter makes me miss you more and that makes it harder to sleep.

I probably told you that already. I find myself repeating many things since you left. Fortunately, I also found out that is perfectly normal and okay!

February 17, 2013

I am fortunate to be surrounded by caring people, and as much as I want one of them to be you, I know that is just not possible. I hold your memories close to my heart and I have your photos everywhere. Oh Sweetie, I never knew empty until I didn't have you. (Is that a song?)

I went to early church this morning so I could go to a rag rug making class at Swanstone Gardens ~ it was my therapy today. Some girls from work came to make rugs, too, and offer moral support—I need that!

February 23, 2013, 10:45 p.m.

Sweetie, I've got your pillow all laid out next to me so I can feel like you're beside me. I know you are in my heart and I can sense your presence, but physically I don't want to feel so alone. I hope everyone experiences a love like ours—one where they know the other "can't live without them." That has such new meaning for me now, darling, because the "can't live without you" has lost the physical component.

You are all around me. I am surrounded by memories. It was good for me that I loved you and oh so good for me that you loved me right back. People say when I talk about you, they can just hear and see how much I loved you. I hope they know how much you loved me, too.

March 1, 2013, 9:47 p.m.

I got a postcard in the mail on the next grief support class. I will go as it really helps. Never knew how hard it was to lose the one you love—wish I didn't know now.

March 6, 2013, 3:42 a.m.

I'm trying to be a little more productive. I want to get things done, but it is challenging because I miss you, because it is our home and I am here without you. It is just empty without you.

I never envisioned my life without you.

Deborah Young

Chapter 11

Help Me Find Myself

One afternoon when I worked in the nursing home, I hurried to get to the time clock so I could punch in on time. My intention to slide quickly past the group of residents sitting outside the dining room had been foiled by an insistent tug on the leg of my white pants. Stopping in my tracks, I looked down to see a wrinkled hand with paper-thin skin desperately hanging onto me.

Monica, her face surrounded by a bevy of white curls, looked up at me, her blue-gray eyes pleading. "Can you help me?" she begged in a shaky voice.

"Sure, Monica. What do you need?" I asked as I knelt down next to her wheelchair so I would be at her eye level.

"Can you help me find myself?" she asked.

"Why, Monica, you are right here," I said as I gently squeezed her hand. In her eyes, I could see an emptiness, perhaps even fear.

"No," she answered as she emphatically shook her head. "This is my body, but I'm not in here anymore."

Today without my husband, I felt like Monica. Physically, I appeared to be the same, but inside, my soul and spirit felt crushed. Uncertainties swirled in my head. Who am I? How can I be a "me" when

I've always been an "us." That hollow feeling returned.

Rolling over in bed, I repositioned Willie's pillow, punching it down out of frustration as much as to get it in the right position.

Who am I?

How strange that I had to ask myself that question.

Who am I? A mother. Ah, part of parents. A grandmother. One half of grandparents. A neighbor. The couple next door. Ugh! Flipping over in the bed, I covered my head with the velour blanket. Tears wet the pillow.

I lay there letting time lapse. I replayed the words I'd heard in my grief class: "You must accept the fact that you're single."

Single. I did not like that.

Single. Accept the harsh reality that death ended your marriage. Harsh words. I shook my head.

Embrace the positives. Really? How did they expect me to do that? Were there any positives?

Redefine yourself, they said. Develop your own values and beliefs.

Single they said.

Sitting up in the bed, I found my journal in the pile of books on the headboard and opened it to a blank page. At the top, I wrote down "I am . . ." Willie and I had many common interests, but we also did things on our own. Certainly, I could find myself with a list.

Daughter, sister, aunt, cousin, niece—more than a wife. Flea market gardener, reader, writer, painter, crossword solver—a hobbyist. Physical therapist assistant, co-worker, teacher, facilitator, exercise instructor—an employee. Friend, church member, Christian, child of God—loved.

Loved.

I closed the journal and lie back on the bed.

Loved.

I didn't know how, but I knew I could go on. God had not abandoned me and I needed to trust Him.

So do not fear, for I am with you; do not be dismayed,
for I am your God. I will strengthen you and help you;
I will uphold you with my righteous right hand.
Isaiah 41:10

March 7, 2013, 9:58 a.m.

I miss you, Sweetie. I even miss that darn coffee cup you always left on the table. Funny how that seems so insignificant now. Who would have thought I'd miss all those annoying little things?

March 10, 2013, 10:55 p.m.

Time sprung ahead today—on the clocks anyway. It's still dragging for me.

March 29, 2013, 10:16 p.m.

Hey, Sweetie. My sleep schedule is all screwed up again. It doesn't seem to be working without you. Sometimes I can close my eyes and feel the touch of your hand on my hip, taste the cherry ChapStick on your lips, smell your coconut shampoo, see your devilish grin, and hear you breathe. But I know it is all a dream and it makes my heart ache so.

April 2, 2013, 10:03 p.m.

Well, Sweetie, I managed to get out of bed and even drove Jazzy to the bus stop and went to the grocery store before work. It was on my way to work that I realized I never fixed my hair. It's good to laugh!

April 3, 2013, 6:00 a.m.

We always joked about having the bed to ourselves, but it is really empty without you. You always told me that when I traveled without you, but I didn't want to know how right you were.

Took your name off of more things yesterday. I hate those tasks—it is so final—and real. Something tells me this isn't a bad dream.

The Son Rises

Ah, a quiet morning. Rising just before five o'clock to feed Tootsie, I had every intention of going back to bed. I saw a few things that needed to be done and the next thing I knew, the clock read nearly six. Resolved to staying out of bed, I put on some coffee, a once-daily activity that seldom occurred now.

After setting my black "Coffee with my Sweetie" cup on the counter, I busied myself while I waited. I moved the mug so I could wipe off the countertop. I caught a glimpse of a picture of Willie and me standing in front of the garden shed, and I smiled. Brenda and Alexia had selected the photos and gave the cup to me on my wedding anniversary, their way of bringing Willie back to me that day.

Once the coffee finished brewing, I poured a cup and headed in the living room to curl up with my computer. No sweetie here to lie next to in bed while we drank our coffee and discussed our plans for the day. Now while I sipped at my coffee or tea, I checked the computer to see what went on in everyone else's lives.

The less-than-perfect routine helped me feel not so alone. Some "Words with Friends" games to play, some new pictures to look at and status updates to peruse. After that, I could write some more about this journey that seemed to have no end. I sighed. When would I begin enjoying the coming of a new day again?

Suddenly, I heard footsteps on the stairs and thought one of my granddaughters had risen. Imagine my surprise when I saw the sleepy head of my son emerge from the stairway. Keep in mind, my son is a typical young man, one that stays up nearly all night and probably went to bed just prior to his mother rising for the day.

"What are you doing up? Do you know what time it is?" I laughed.

"Yeah, I know. I had a weird dream, really weird, and I needed to see if you were alright," he said as he ran his hand through his hair.

I could discern the look of concern on his face. "I'm just fine, kiddo. Just fine," I told him. "Are you alright?"

"Yeah. I just needed to know you were okay, so now I am going back to bed." He turned and headed back up the stairs.

Poor kid. I thought it best not to ask him about the weird dream. I felt I knew already. I'd seen that look before, the morning his father had passed away, and my heart ached. That morning the really weird dream was anything but a dream.

> *Therefore we do not lose heart ... So we fix our eyes not on what is seen, but on what is unseen. For what is seen is temporary, but what is unseen is eternal.*
> *2 Corinthians 4:16a,18*

April 6, 2013, 7:30 a.m.

I don't have the drive I used to have when you were here with me. I guess we don't realize what strength we draw from each other until one of us isn't here.

April 7, 2013, 11:12 p.m.

I attended another grief class—still can't talk about losing you without tears falling. It's okay though—they are cleansing apparently.

April 11, 2013, 10:14 p.m.

Wish it didn't hurt so much to lose you. I never saw this coming.

April 14, 2013, 9:52 p.m.

Actually cleaned up the kitchen today. Quite an accomplishment as I don't clean much. I just don't care.

April 29, 2013, 3:51 a.m.

I was happy to find two of your curly gray hairs on one of your shirts. Probably seems crazy, but that was one thing I never thought I'd do again—run my fingers through your hair, so I just ran my fingers over them and thought about how much I loved your curly locks. I put them in the little wooden box on the nightstand. I want to save them.

May 1, 2013, 4:28 a.m.

Reached out for you this morning, but no matter how far I reached, you weren't there. People keep telling me this will get easier, but I am not so sure. Seems I miss you more and more each day. The days are long without you and yet I get nothing done. I hope and pray that I can find half the happiness that you have in heaven.

I think I am still kicking myself, too. All those worries I had about you—the signs I could see with your balance and memory and mood—and the doctors weren't concerned, but I knew something was wrong.

Do I ever feel powerless.

May 27, 2013, 10:16 p.m.

I went to the Shawano Flea Market yesterday and I really missed you—not just so you could carry my stuff, either! Missed sharing ideas with you and pointing out cool wooden boxes or cast iron. I did hear some funny stories about you. Guess you can still make me laugh.

The Touch of His Hand

Willie and I had traveled to Michigan, where we located an out-of-the-way antique shop in an old red barn. We entered the shop through the large sliding doors together, and as usual, Willie headed in one direction and I in another. I made one walk-through and then a second, finding a few treasures for myself, but still in search of my husband. I found him in the back of the barn, bent over a drab-looking, wooden tea and coffee canister that stood approximately 30 inches high.

Willie's parents had been antique dealers and he inherited their love for old things. Hence, it became one of our favorite pastimes. We included visits to flea markets or antique shops on the itinerary wherever we went. On such treasure hunts, I'd often find him running his hand over a rusty piece of cast iron or a worn wooden piece, with a longing in his eyes. I saw that yearning now.

"There you are, Sweetie! Are you about ready to go?" I asked.

"Did you see this?" He lifted the container and set it on the edge of a nearby milk can.

I tried to muster up some enthusiasm. From my vantage point, I saw nothing outstanding about this wooden cylinder. "No, I didn't."

He tipped the can back and rubbed his fingers across the dusty label. "You see that?" In red print, I could make out "Young Bros," and knew this piece would be coming home with us.

He sat the canister back up and ran his fingers along the dull metal strip that highlighted the seam. He sat it back on the ground, where he took the lid off and put it back on. He picked it up and flipped it over, carefully checking the bottom all the way around. His fingers touched every bit of the wooden container as though reading a story in Braille. Satisfied, he headed to the register, carrying this dusty wooden can whose lackluster metal strip ran from top to bottom while I wondered what had become of my husband's sanity.

When we arrived home, Willie wasted no time in tending to his "treasure." He carefully dusted it with a rag that formerly had been a T-shirt. He used the sander on the wood, first with a medium grit paper and then finishing it off with a finer one. Each time, he'd gently run his fingers over each inch. When it felt just right, the T-shirt dust rag came out again.

Next, Willie rigged up a contraption to support the round cylinder while he varnished it. Brush bristles, dipped slowly into the can of polyurethane and wiped at its edge, gently glided from one end of the canister to the other. One coat would dry and he would turn the canister to apply varnish in another area until a gleaming coat shone all the way around. Between coats, he hand-sanded and started the process over again. Patient with his work, Willie spent many hours revealing the beauty hidden in this particular wooden can.

With the canister finished, I could see the vision my husband had seen all along. The grain of the wood boasted fine lines. The metal seam showed off a glorious aged patina. The greens, reds, and golds of the coffee label stood out brilliantly. Even the metal staples around the rim of the lid shouted "look at me!" I ran my fingers over the surfaces. Willie's eyes sparkled. We had a beautiful antique for our home.

Goosebumps jolted me back to the present as I realized my memories were not random thoughts, but lessons from God. Willie saw a beauty in that canister that most people, including me, had overlooked, similar to the way God sees the unique benefits in each situation. The grief I was experiencing gave me rough edges that needed to be sanded down. I needed the touch of the Master's hand.

God could pick up my pieces and dust them off if I would let Him. Trusting God and allowing Him to use my hardship would be the key to smoothing out the surfaces and feeling polished once again. God is patient. He knows through his attention to details that one day I will understand the vision He already sees.

> *For we are God's workmanship, created in Christ Jesus to do good works, which God prepared in advance for us to do. Ephesians 2:10*

Chapter 12

Coming to Terms
With the "W" Word

They sat in wooden chairs with cushioned seats. They sat on a light-colored sofa. They sat on overstuffed arm chairs. Everyone had been arranged in a horseshoe so I could stand in the center, where I could be seen and heard by all.

After glancing around the room, I focused on the paper in my hand. All of us had at least one thing in common and I dared not make eye contact. It would be hard to speak if I broke down, and today's gathering had been intended to heal.

We were a club, a support group. We were friends and strangers. We were women and widows.

Seven months had elapsed and the word continued to stick in my throat. If only I had perfected an invitation to a widow's luncheon that excluded that "W" word, I could go on forever and not utter it.

During week three of GriefShare, discussion focused on losing one's spouse. I hated the session. Single became the word of the day and I had no idea how to do that. Willie and I had plans—adventures, travels, bike rides, growing old—together! He had been mine twenty-four hours a day for nearly thirty years, and now they're telling me not to act like I died, too.

"Remember, marriage is no longer your identity," Curtis said.

"I remember when I had to go change my W-2 forms," Sally said. "It was one of the hardest things I had to do and I just had to check a box . . . the single box."

"I didn't even think about doing that," I said.

"I went home afterwards and painted the bathroom," Sally said as she laughed.

"I painted the hallway after Willie passed," I said, and we both laughed.

When I left GriefShare, I spent time sitting in the car. I threw my book and purse on the black-covered passenger seat, leaned my head back into the headrest and closed my eyes. I could smell the leather. Usually the sessions renewed my strength and confirmed I had not lost my mind, but today's zapped my spirit. No matter what they said, I contended that I continued to be Mrs. Young. In my heart, I was as married as the day I said "I do."

The week's homework didn't fare much better and I struggled with it. What needs did I have? Did I feel empty? Lonely? Did I have unfulfilled dreams? Wow. I lost my best friend and now they were asking me stupid questions including when did I miss Willie?

When did I miss him? I missed him most in the morning, in the morning. I missed him most in the evening, in the evening. I pulled a piece of scrap paper off the headboard and began writing a poem.

The next weekend, the GriefShare meeting commenced at the usual time. Curtis began to jump right into the next session.

"Curtis, I had a hard time with last week's session and I just want to share a poem I wrote as part of the homework," I said.

No one spoke as I read "I Miss You Most." The tears that rolled down cheeks told me others had similar experiences.

"Wow. Would you be willing to read that at the Widow's Luncheon?" Curtis asked.

So here I stood, in front of a roomful of widows, sharing my heart and soul. Reality set in.

I am that "W" word.

> *The king asked her, "What is troubling you?" She said,*
> *"I am indeed a widow; my husband is dead."*
> *2 Samuel 14:5*

May 28, 2013, 9:45 p.m.

The tulips that I planted behind the playhouse about five years ago, the ones that never bloomed, actually bloomed this year on Mother's Day. I was certain they were a gift from you. Tonight I looked up the meaning of tulips—remembrance and determination. How cool is that, Sweetie?

June 3, 2013, 10:51 p.m.

Nearly eleven, Sweetie, and I am just now coming to bed. Long day today with yard work and gardening, not to mention Jazzy started playing ball. Lots of work to do to get ready for the blessing and memorial garden dedication. Much much work, but you know I love it outside—just miss you and your constant interruptions!

June 21, 2013, 10:40 p.m.

Tomorrow's the day, Sweetie. You'll be in the garden at last. Bittersweet. Everything is always bittersweet! I want you in your resting place, but the finality of it all. Damn. It's so hard sometimes.

Blessing and Memorial Garden Dedication

The urn sat next to the dresser, the same space it had occupied since Christmas when it needed to be moved to make a spot to put the tree. Each morning, I traced the letters of Willie's name with my fingertips.

Unlike a magic lamp, nothing appeared as I rubbed the surface. Yet, I still felt the need to make physical contact with the urn as though that somehow connected Willie and me once again. My heart continued to ache. Not only did I miss my sweetie, but now I had relegated him to a dusty corner. The time had come to place Willie's urn in the memorial garden.

I wanted to have his graveside service. The ashes needed to be blessed even though I knew my sweetie had already gone on to a new life; I needed that for me. People should be part of the service and share a meal, joining together in a celebration of the blessings in our life.

Our two youngest children agreed with the idea, and before long we scheduled a date with the pastor and sent out announcements. Discussions ensued on what the service should include. More discussions took place on menu options. Other discussions centered on what else we would need.

Rachael would borrow tables from work. Bud and Carl, our neighbor, would work together to pour the cement for the urn. I started a to-do list and a grocery list. In the last eight months, I had learned I needed lots of lists. I breathed a sigh of relief. At last, my sweetie would be in his resting place.

The garden itself had to be tended to. While it still contained touches of him through his work boots, cast iron kettle, farm machinery, and coffee house bird house, I had received gifts specifically for the garden, gifts of angels and stepping stones. A concrete statue of a man holding a lantern also awaited placement in the garden. All of the gifts should be in the garden prior to the service.

A garden wouldn't be a garden without plants. The hardy mums, traditionally an autumn flower, had been planted last fall. Daylilies, including Angels on High, already grew along the back edge of the memorial garden. Willie was called home in the fall, so I wanted to stick to fall colors. I transplanted pale orange pansies into Willie's work boots. Pansies, flowers of remembrance that also symbolize union and togetherness, seemed a perfect selection for the garden. Next, red and orange marigolds added color around the front border of the garden. Marigolds symbolize grief. I planted lots of marigolds! Lastly, yellow loosestrife, set to bloom in the month of June when the blessing and garden dedication would occur, inserted color on either side of the engraved stepping stone. The garden came together at last.

The day of the service, I woke early. One more thing needed to be placed in the garden: the urn. After a quick shower, I carried the urn from the bedroom to the backyard. The tools on the picnic table told me my neighbor had also risen. He appeared around the corner of the house.

"Good morning," Carl said. "Did you want to put that in now?"

"If there is anything that is going to go wrong today that will ruin this day for me, it's that the urn doesn't go in like it is supposed to. I need it in now," I replied.

Reluctantly, I handed over the urn. Though it needed to be placed in the garden, I still found it difficult to put it in someone else's hands. The trial fitting did not go well. My heart hurt. Upbeat and positive, Carl said, "It just needs a few adjustments." He disappeared back around the corner and soon returned with more tools. He began chipping away and in a short time, the urn slid easily into place.

"Do you know which way is north?" I asked.

We looked this way and that. "I think north is this way, but I'm not sure," Carl said.

Apparently, we were both directionally disoriented. "I just thought it would be nice if the sundial worked. Willie was always a hard worker, so I thought he could keep working," I said.

Carl looked around again. "Well, it might be this way . . . No, wait. I think it's this way. I guess, I really just don't know," he said.

Folding my arms across my chest, I plopped myself down on the swing. "Fine. Let the man rest!" I said. The urn stayed where it had been placed.

Willie had fabricated a workbench I had wanted to use to place the food on, but even though it was on wheels, it proved difficult to move, especially on the grass. The food could be served from the driveway, but that made for a long way for people to walk back to the tables. The balance of some of my guests worried me, so that would not work. The tables could be moved up between the house and the playhouse, but there was no shade there.

"Guys, can I change my mind again?" I asked. My neighbor and my son exercised much patience with me.

"We can do anything you want," Carl said.

The tables, lined up like soldiers, sat under the only shade tree I had. The folding chairs formed three neat rows by the memorial garden. The food looked inviting on a make-shift table next to the vegetable garden.

In lieu of Willie's workbench, I found other creations that would assist in bringing him home to me for the day. An Encyclopedia Britannica wood crate that he had refinished, placed at the beginning of the food line, made the perfect place to put plates, napkins, and utensils. A refinished Yeast Foam box kept the napkins contained. His Griswold oven, rescued from the basement, took up residency next to the wooden crate and held the bread. At last, I managed to incorporate his spirit into the food line.

To maintain Willie's physical presence the day of the blessing and dedication, my Aunt Estell helped me place black-bordered photo collage posters on top of cream-colored tablecloths. The posters reflected the roles he played in his life so people could see him and what he meant to all of us.

The process of putting the posters together helped me heal. I looked through our photos once again and conjured up memories of the blessed times we shared. I read the headings again as Aunt Estell and I smoothed a clear vinyl tablecloth over them. "Son/Brother," "Dad" and "Gramps, Grandfather, Grandpa."

My favorite signified the relationships he and I shared. He had been so much more than my husband and I wanted the photos under the heading, "Friend, Partner, Confidant, Sweetie, Lover, Spouse, Darling," to reflect that.

Willie would be with everyone no matter where they sat.

People began arriving about a half hour prior to eleven, the time the event had been scheduled to begin. Though things remained undone, it didn't matter as people pitched in and helped pull it all together. No one had been asked to bring anything, yet they came bearing dishes to pass. The food multiplied and I thought this must be how people felt when Jesus fed the five thousand.

Pastor Dave and his wife arrived close to 11:00. "Wowsers, Debbi. There is much fellowship taking place right here in your backyard," Pastor Dave said. "I know we are scheduled for 11:00, but I would encourage this to continue. Is it okay, if we begin about 11:30?"

"That's fine with me. The ceremony will be relatively brief, so I think it is safe to hold off on the start time," I said. Silently, I said a prayer of thanks. The time would allow me a private moment of peace and tranquility.

At 11:30, the group of approximately forty sat in the chairs in front of the memorial garden and the service commenced. Pastor Dave read from Ecclesiastes, Chapter 3.

"There is a time for everything, and a season for every activity under heaven: a time to be born and a time to die, a time to plant and a time to uproot, a time to kill and a time to heal, a time to tear down and a time to build, a time to weep and a time to laugh, a time to mourn and a time to dance, a time to scatter stones and a time to gather them, a time to embrace and a time to refrain, a time to search and a time to give up, a time to keep and a time to throw away, a time to tear and a time to mend, a time to be silent and a time to speak, a time to love and a time to hate, a time for war and a time for peace."

"Shall we bow our heads in prayer?"

After praying together, Pastor Dave shared words of comfort. I could smell the pungent odor of the marigolds, the sweetness of fresh-mowed grass. The smell of rain had passed and I felt grateful. Peach-colored pansies abundantly filled Willie's work boots, which stood like sentries near the base of the urn. Deep emotion swept through me as our daughter, Rachael, sang. Her Daddy loved to hear her sing. A single tear trickled down my cheek and I knew this was the time to let him rest.

Following a prayer of thanksgiving and the Lord's Prayer, everyone filled their plates and headed to the tables. I waited for everyone else to find a seat before sitting down. Behind me, I heard laughter and joy.

"Just look at him," Michelle remarked. "You can just see his sweetness and yet know he was a force to be reckoned with." Everyone at their table giggled.

"I can see why she fell in love with him," Edith said.

I thought about the poster at their table: "Welder, Veteran, Traveler, Demo Derby Driver, Beach Walker, Refinisher, Collector, Packer Fan." The largest picture in that collage showed Willie wearing his welding leathers, his curly red hair and full beard in disarray below a welding helmet flipped up atop his head. I recalled the innocent, yet mischievous look in his eyes and smiled. Even in his photos, the animal magnetism came through.

In the absence of his physical being, his essence resided with us today, and at long last, perhaps we both could rest.

Late in the afternoon the Twelve came to him and said, "Send the crowd away so they can go to the surrounding villages and countryside and find food and lodging, because we are in a remote place here." He replied, "You give them something to eat." They answered, "We have only five loaves of bread and two fish—unless we go and buy food for all this crowd." (About five thousand men were there.) But he said to his disciples, "Have them sit down in groups of about fifty each." The disciples did so, and everybody sat down. Taking the five loaves and the two fish and looking up to heaven, he gave thanks and broke them. Then he gave them to the disciples to set before the people. They all ate and were satisfied, and the disciples picked up twelve basketfuls of broken pieces that were left over. Luke 9: 12-17

June 23, 2013, 4:03 a.m.

Hey, Sweetie—Wee morning hours and I'm awake again. It's different this morning. While I still miss you, I feel content with all the love and support I've received. The ceremony was beautiful yesterday for your blessing and the memorial garden dedication. I am not sure how many people were here, but it was a yard full. Your ashes are resting in the garden now and the gardens are exceptionally beautiful this year. I don't know if I will find peace now or not, but I am at least content. I love you, Sweetie.

June 24, 2013, 10:15 p.m.

Kind of an idle day today. I did not realize how consumed I had been getting things ready for your blessing. It was nice to not have anything pressing to do and just enjoy the gardens. Your urn looks perfect in the garden, and I sat out on the swing and talked with you today. I planted forget-me-nots, both Shirley and Mary Jo brought them to me, and Iona brought me basil. And you know me, I found a place for it all. I miss you, Sweetie. So very, very much.

June 29, 2013, 7:55 a.m.

It is over eight months now and I still cry myself to sleep some nights and I still wake up feeling so empty! Our lives were so intertwined and we loved each other so much. That's why it is so hard to be without you, I guess. It takes approximately eight weeks for a bone to heal; now I know it takes over eight months for a broken heart to heal.

July 8, 2013, 11:52 p.m.

I am painting a garden post on Saturday. I thought I could paint one side with cast iron, one with moon and stars, etc., as a memorial post for you. Rachael said I need to paint it for me. She said I have been so focused on doing things for you that now I just need to do something for me and that's okay. Maybe I do. It's just so hard!

July 19, 2013, 2:23 a.m.

Why do I wake up in the middle of the night missing you? And more yet, how long will this go on? It's been nine months—nine months and I still miss you like crazy! I always thought it was bad when we were apart for a few days and now I don't know how long until we are together again. Sometimes I just close my eyes and I can feel your hand on my hip. I can see your smile, hear your breath. I miss you.

July 27, 2013, 10:48 p.m.

Just read a few love notes from you. I always loved to find the notes you left for me. They made my day. I guess they still do.

Chapter 13

Love Notes

I lay on my left side on the massage table with my right arm stretched up over the side of my head. The pain hit suddenly then, and I could feel the tears welling up in my eyes. I shut them tightly, bit my lower lip, and did exactly what I tell my patients not to do—held my breath.

I relaxed a bit as the hurt let up, but it didn't subside long. My right arm curled farther around my head and I gripped the end of the table with my hand. Though I couldn't see them, I knew my knuckles had whitened.

As the smarting sensation eased again, I loosened my grip and gently shut my eyes. I prayed it wouldn't last much longer. The smell of rubbing alcohol invaded my nostrils and the bright fluorescent lighting forced me to keep my eyes closed.

"You're doing great," Wade assured me. "The outline is almost done."

My eyes were wide open then. The outline? The outline. I couldn't believe the color hadn't even been started yet, and suddenly I wondered how my friends' simple suggestion had even gone this far.

I thought back to that warm summer day. Gathered together around my backyard picnic table, we worked on our toothbrush rag rugs. It always proved to be a great time to share our anguishes and our triumphs.

"Guess what I found?" I asked, not waiting for an answer. "A note from Willie." They all stopped working on their rugs, grabbed their half full wine glasses, and stared at me.

I continued, "I don't remember him writing it, so I don't really know if it's from him or a gift from heaven."

"Go on," Sue said, her eyes getting bigger.

"For no specific reason, I was having a particularly bad day. Bud and I had been driving around and stopped at the Shell station to get gas. He pumped the gas and for some reason, I felt the need to look through my wallet. Inside, I found a small folded piece of paper with Willie's handwriting on it."

"Well, what did it say?" Heather asked.

I pulled it out of my bag. "I am always with you, even when I am not here. Love ya, Willie." I sat back in my chair and smiled as I took a drink of my wine.

"That just gives me goose bumps," Terry said. And the others nodded in agreement.

We sipped our Moscato and reveled in the divine moment.

Sue broke the silence. "You should put that on a tattoo." Heather and Terry agreed.

"I don't know," I said. I resumed working on the rug, lovingly transforming Willie's T-shirts into something new. "Where would you put it? I mean, if you did get a tattoo?"

Wade's voice brought me back to the present. "Try not to turn away from me." I had opted to get Willie's words tattooed on my right side, along the iliac crest, the place he had always placed his hand when we lie in bed together. Along with his words, two purple pansies for remembrance, union, and togetherness. Wade had suggested three buds to represent our children, which seemed like a good idea at the time. The throbbing intensified and I bit my lower lip.

"You're doing great." Wade tried to encourage me. "We're starting on the color now. Just hang in there."

I closed my eyes and wondered if this decision had been one of those rash ones they tell you not to make in the first year. I still worked at the same clinic. I still lived in the same house. I hadn't married again. I hadn't even dated. But could a tattoo, something I never thought I'd do, be considered impulsive?

Oh! I cried out as the stinging increased again. A tattoo over the bone? Had I been thinking at all?

I prayed. "Dear Lord, how you must have suffered! The pain as they nailed you to the cross, as the sword pierced your side. I am so weak. Thank you for dying for me, for believing in my worth, for loving me. Be with me, Lord. Give me the strength I need. Help me to humble myself, to acknowledge that I cannot do this without you. I don't think I ever realized how truly great your sacrifice until this very moment."

Wade continued to work diligently as I lie on my left side. I loosened the grip I had on the table as I pondered the emotional pain I had suffered over the last ten months—how certain it seemed that life would not go on, how sorry I had felt for myself because the dreams I had had for the future were crushed. All paled in comparison to what Jesus had done.

With or without a tattoo, Willie's mark had been left on me. But more importantly, Jesus had marked me.

> *And being found in appearance as a man, he humbled himself and became obedient to death— even death on a cross! Philippians 2:8*

July 29, 2013, 10:43 p.m.

Somber day today. Some days I miss you so much and I can't get myself motivated to do much of anything. The house is empty without you here and it is a reminder of lost dreams—our dreams.

August 6, 2013, 3:23 a.m.

Wee hours of the morning and I am thinking about what I'll do when I get up. I prepared zucchini for freezing the other day, but I didn't have any eggs for making bread, so I just may do that. I loved when I'd bake a treat and you'd come in the kitchen asking, "Can we eat that?" I was always sure to have enough for you because you were so cute asking. I love how you can still make me smile, Sweetie.

Always with me—just like your note says.

I went and had my hair cut again yesterday, too. Yeah, yeah. I know you don't like it short, but it is all I can manage right now.

I better try to go back to sleep.

August 17, 2013, 10:52 p.m.

Do you know I have not stopped sleeping on your side of the bed? It makes me feel closer to you somehow. I can hear you say, "Git on your own side of the bed!" but I won't. I'll stay right here on your side, because I need to sense your presence, feel your love and comfort. Can you tell how much I miss you?

Pity Party Mondays

Ugh! 9:07. Twenty minutes since the last time I checked. I set the clock back down on the headboard and flung the red quilt aside, reluctantly sitting up on the edge of the bed. Most of the night had been spent tossing and turning . . . again.

Do the next thing. So easy for them to say. I rolled my eyes and shook my head.

"At least it's Monday," I said to no one in particular. Widows don't have anyone to talk to in the morning.

Monday. No work. No church. No place I have to go. No demands made on me so I could do anything I wanted.

Once I donned my robe, I went to the bathroom.

Just doing the next thing.

I came out of the bathroom and thought about breakfast. Willie would have taken me out. We'd order French toast and a mushroom and cheese omelet with a side of crisp bacon. We'd share. We'd sip hazelnut coffee and lay out our plans for the day. I could almost smell the aromas of hazelnut and bacon.

I vetoed breakfast. Instead, I plopped myself down in the recliner and pulled a quilt up around me. The nearest I'd get to a hug today.

Plans for the day played out in my mind. No getting dressed. No going out. I'd just sit right here in this chair with my box of tissues and think about how much I missed Willie.

In ten months of Mondays, the routine altered only due to some external force. An appointment—medical, legal, insurance—or a person—child, friend, co-worker—thinking I spent too much time alone.

But blue Mondays had turned into my favorite days—and my most unproductive ones.

Settling into the recliner, I pulled the quilt up even tighter and turned my head to the right, an ideal position to do nothing. Nothing at all.

I closed my eyes for a moment, wishing my husband back, wishing we had gone together. My heart hurt. Opening my eyes, I saw the sun shining. How dare it. I averted my gaze and spotted a maroon-covered book on the coffee table. In gold letters, all capitals, it said, "Holy Bible."

During the sermon yesterday, Pastor Dave suggested reading Hebrews 11 and 12. I reached for the Bible and read. When I finished the passage, I cried. The tears? Different somehow.

"God, surely if You took care of all those people whose troubles had been so great, You'll take care of me."

Suddenly, I tossed the quilt aside and returned the recliner to its original position. The clock proclaimed the eleven o'clock hour. On Mondays, our church held a service at a local nursing home just after one o'clock and had a need for volunteers. I quickly dressed and actually brushed my teeth before noon. As I walked over to the nursing home,

I felt renewed. The warm air felt good against my skin and the birds singing lifted my spirits.

I paused a moment before entering Bornemann Nursing Home. How many times had I walked right past these doors, giving no thought to who resided here? I pulled the door open and entered. Inside, I talked with Laurie, the activity director. This petite woman with medium-length blond hair greeted me with a smile.

"No. Nothing special you have to do. Just come back around one o'clock and you can help us bring residents down to the chapel," she said. Her smile made me feel wanted, useful.

"I'll be here," I answered.

I reported back to the nursing home, and with Laurie's guidance, assisted parishioners to the weekly service. My duties included passing out hymnals, singing praises, and sharing in the service. Physically, I touched people, but inside, God let them awaken my spirit, my love for Him and His creations.

Week two, I delighted in knowing I had purpose. At 12:55, I reported to the nursing home, eager to be of service again. As I entered, I saw her sitting there, in a reclining wheelchair parked on a speckled terrazzo floor, in the mint-green tiled corridor. Silver curls enveloped a face, yellowed from healing bruises. Tubing from a nasal cannula supplied her oxygen from the tank attached to the back of the chair. Her frail hands, covered with nearly transparent skin, folded together neatly in front of her and held midway between her lap and her chin. It reminded me of my own grandmother. Her aquamarine eyes glistened, wet with tears.

"Mary, are you crying?" a staff member asked.

"Yes." Mary's voice quivered.

"What's the matter, Mary?" asked the staff member, leaning in toward Mary as though to comfort her.

"Nothing's wrong," Mary responded. "These are tears of joy."

"Joy?" The staff member, a puzzled expression on her face, knelt beside Mary. "What are you happy about?"

"My blessings, of course. My family and friends and everything I have," Mary said.

In that brief exchange, I realized for months my focus had been on what I didn't have: my husband. My focus required a shift onto the many blessings God bestowed upon me.

I love Mondays. Beautiful, spirit-filled Mondays. There truly is joy in serving others.

Each of you should look not only to your own interests,
but also to the interests of others. Philippians 2:4

August 18, 2013, 6:02 a.m.

Good morning, Sweetie ~

Today marks ten months since God took you home. Ten long and lonely months on a journey I never planned to take. You know it hasn't been easy for me, but you? You are with your Lord and Savior! You are pain-free. You don't have to work so hard anymore. I am happy for you.

I pray often for God's guidance and strength. He's given all that to me and more. I would not be where I am today without Him, and I know you know that, Sweetie.

August 24, 2013, 4:55 a.m.

Good morning, Sweetie ~

Up early again today. My mind wanders to you so often. So many things I'm remembering about you teach me lessons about God—your patience, your faith, your trust—things that were there all the time, but it seems through your death and my increasing faith, the blinders have come off and I am able to make these connections. Perhaps today, I shall go sit by the pond at the Wildlife Sanctuary amidst God's creations.

Trust and Faith Bring Him Back to Me

I sat on the smooth surface of the rock at the water's edge, beneath a tree with heart shaped leaves. The water stood still except for a few small areas where the ripples reminded me of my husband's curls. I closed my eyes and the rustle of the leaves reminded me of the playing cards we used to attach to our bicycle tires with wooden clothespins. The last bicycle ride I had with my husband had been on our tandem bicycle, no playing card and no wooden clothespin.

The day he bought that bicycle, I had come home from work and found him happily shifting his weight back and forth in the back entryway. "Come over here and see what I got for us," he eagerly said.

Imagine my surprise when I saw a shiny red and white two-seater Schwinn sitting in the backyard. I ran my hand over the signature "S" on the seat. We had never discussed getting a tandem bicycle. We had discussed my husband getting more exercise. I raised my eyebrows at Willie. "I thought we could exercise together," he commented. How blessed I was.

Our first rides together became true tests of trust. Willie, his six-foot-one frame quite a bit bigger than mine, sat in the front, blocking my view over and around him. I placed all my faith in him, hoping and praying that he led me on the right paths. The more we rode, the more the trust grew.

When fall arrived, Willie promised me a drive to see the autumn colors. Weeks passed and the leaves changed color and began to fall from the trees. I reminded my husband more than a few times about our drive.

One Sunday afternoon, I worked in the kitchen with my apron donned and my hands in a sink full of dirty dish water. I heard Willie exit out the back door. Before long, I heard a knock on the front door. Knowing my husband had just left, I dried my hands and went to answer it. When I opened the door, I found Willie standing there.

"Darling, what are you doing?" I asked.

He took a step back and extended his hand. "You said I promised you a drive to look at the fall colors." There sat our tandem bicycle, all ready to go.

"Darling, I . . . I thought . . . I meant . . . "

"C'mon," he said. "Where's your sense of adventure?"

I tossed my apron aside and put on my tennis shoes. The time for a drive to see those fall colors had arrived. We took the bike trails back through Baird Creek. We saw the brilliant oranges, the raging reds, and the tantalizing yellows. The colors never looked more beautiful.

We heard the crunch of the leaves beneath the bicycle tires, something we never would have experienced in a vehicle. As we worked together on that bicycle, I knew this was the best ride to see the fall colors I had ever experienced. Being in nature with the man I loved felt perfect. My trust and faith in him grew strong.

Sitting here on this rock next to the water, my knees bent up to my chest, I could feel a tear trickle down my cheek as I recalled those events. I closed my eyes and a gentle breeze brushed the hair back from my face much like Willie had done so many times before. The breeze strengthened and it felt as though Willie had his entire arms wrapped around me, but I knew in my heart, it was God's loving arms.

My faith and trust in God grew strong. Willie and I had never sat here in this place together until now.

> *Trust in the Lord forever, for the Lord, the Lord, is the Rock eternal. Isaiah 26:4*

August 31, 2013, 3:41 a.m.

Good morning, Sweetie. Can't seem to get back to sleep. Thinking about every day with you—the way you sat at the table with your coffee and your newspaper, your smile as you told me about your plans for the day, the feel of your lips on my cheek when you gave me a kiss as you left the kitchen to get dressed.

Sometimes I wear your robe ~ and yes, the sleeves are rolled up! Sometimes I wear one of your denim shirts. Anything that is yours makes me feel close to you.

I plan to start refinishing the living room floor today. It's a big job and I can see why you put it off, but I'll be happy with it when it's done. So glad you taught me about refinishing. Not sure I'd tackle such a big job without that knowledge!

September 9, 2013, 3:30 a.m.

Wee morning hours again. I think so often about how much I miss you. It is tough living out our dreams without you. I want to be happy and I am, but part of me is still sad. I'm still working on the living room. Everything takes time and I suppose I need that. Stay busy or pout over losing you.

God is with me every day and I know I have not been abandoned. It is through Him that I draw any ounce of strength I have. I ask for His guidance in all I do.

September 15, 2013, 10:37 p.m.

Sometimes there is not enough things to keep me busy. My tears fall when the sun goes down and I am all alone. Will I ever stop missing you?

Money in the Bank

I sat on the basement steps and let out a heavy sigh as I looked over my husband's so-called money in the bank. He had refinished antiques, and before me sat all the projects he stockpiled for his retirement. Whenever he'd come home with new treasures and I'd give him one of those looks that all guys are familiar with, he'd hug me and say, "It's all money in the bank, Sweetie." I felt overwhelmed looking at the seemingly never-ending piles of stuff.

"I don't know, dear, but from where I am sitting, money in the bank would have been a whole lot easier," I said to no one in particular. My dear had gone home, leaving all of this for me.

As I wrapped my arms around my shoulders to soften the chill, I caught a glimpse of sunlight being reflected off the rim of a can and looked closer—two cans of polyurethane varnish along with sandpaper in two grades and brushes piled together. Ah yes, another one of my husband's unfinished projects. I couldn't count the number of years he promised to get at refinishing that living room floor. The hardwood needed some TLC to revive its beauty. The supplies had all been purchased last fall, a step in the right direction. The thought stirred up the smells of freshly sanded wood and wet varnish.

But God's plans weren't our plans and he called my husband home, leaving me sitting here among all the one-day projects that needed to get done and I doubted I could do it all.

I looked at the supplies for the floor again. I could haul that stuff back to the store and get my money refunded. That would be something cleaned up. Thoughts raced through my mind. I had always wanted that floor done and had been so delighted that he planned to get it done.

The best laid plans.

I sighed again and closed my eyes, lost in the thoughts of our hopes. Our dreams.

Suddenly, I opened my eyes and sat up a little taller. I always wanted that floor done. I allowed the words to swirl in my head like seasoning in soup.

I always wanted that floor done.

With the things Willie had taught me about refinishing, I could refinish that floor. Sure, this was not a piece of furniture or an old shipping crate, but an entire floor. Still, they all had a common denominator. All had been made of well-worn wood.

Unaware of the true nature of this undertaking, I headed upstairs and began clearing the furniture out of the living room. Everything found a temporary home except the couch and love seat, so I sold them. The only condition had been to take them while I worked to spare me the emotional finality of it.

After securing plastic over the doorway to the kitchen, I held my husband's sander in my hands as I knelt on my hands and knees and began sanding the living room floor. A mask covered my mouth and nose to keep me from breathing in the dust, but I could smell the freshness that had been trapped in the wood.

The sander whirred, stirring up memories of Willie teaching me to restore hidden beauty. I saw him with our son as a toddler as he taught him to sand on a wooden trunk. I saw him working side-by-side with our now young adult son last summer as they prepared for an antique show. I saw his smile as he proudly handed me the latest project he had finished. I sat back on my legs, brushing the hair from my face with the sleeve of his beige flannel. What had I been thinking?

Three days later, with the sanding complete, I brewed a pot of coffee. That would have been how Willie would start his work day. "Starting the varnishing today, Sweetie. You'd like how it is looking."

With the can of varnish opened, I started in the corner by the front door. The smell of the polyurethane varnish invaded the room quickly, and I placed a box fan in the window to help dispel the odor.

"Hey, Ma," Bud called from the plastic-covered doorway. "It smells like the van when we loaded up for the Elkhorn show."

I smiled. Willie sold his refurbished wares at the Elkhorn Flea Market four times a year. It became a family affair, a mini-vacation, and an opportunity to work together as we loaded and unloaded the van, sometimes the truck, setting up and tearing down for his day in the sun. Customers raved about the skill he demonstrated in his goods and they all had to touch his items.

"I put the fan in the window to try to tone it down," I said.

"I always kind of liked that smell," Bud said and smiled.

The project continued. A coat of varnish, a sanding. Repeat. Two weeks later, I stood in the doorway, admiring the revived wooden floor.

"Looking good, Ma," Bud said as he came up behind me.

"I think so," I said as I sipped my coffee.

Bud squatted down and ran his hand over the newly varnished surface. "You want to know what Dad would say?" he asked.

"The touch test?" I raised my eyebrows.

"He'd say it needs another coat," Bud said.

I rolled my eyes, but I knew I would be applying another coat. No project was complete until it passed Willie's touch test.

Once the final coat had been applied, I sat back on my legs, looking over what I hoped was a finished floor. I rubbed my right knee to ease the aching pain.

"Lord, I am so grateful to have a floor to work on. Willie would never have been able to refinish this floor. I spent a lot of time on my hands and knees, time in contorted positions. The pain he had in his knees and his left wrist would have escalated if he had to complete this, robbing him of happy days. As it was, You gave me purpose, time to relive precious memories, and count the blessings You have provided me with. Amen."

As with all things, I learned patience and understanding. I learned sometimes it is not about money in the bank, but about the gifts you've been given that makes you believe you can do something you never thought you could.

Give thanks in all circumstances, for this is God's will
for you in Christ Jesus. 1 Thessalonians 5:18

September 18, 2013, 4:04 a.m.

Eleven months today. I count them like we did a baby's age, only this is not as much fun. I'm surviving and my first thought is I don't know how, but I realize I do. God provides the strength to get out of bed each day and the strength to give when I only want to take.

My heart aches for the loss of my Sweetie and rejoices as he enjoys his life in heaven. I think it was too soon, but God? His timing is perfect.

One day I hope to understand. One day I hope sleep comes as easily as God called you home. One day I hope I'll be excited again for mornings, for falls, for fresh-brewed coffee, and a crossword puzzle.

Today is not that day.

October 14, 2013

I am trying to tidy things up so they are easier for me to take care of on my own. Oh, how I hate to think of that! If things were reversed, I'd want you to be happy, to move forward, but somehow I can't make myself do it! If you weren't so much of me, weren't entwined in everything I do, maybe it would be easier, but I doubt it.

I am glad I had the chance to love you and be loved by you. Some people go their whole lives and don't have that kind of love, but we were the lucky ones, because we did have each other.

I love you, Sweetie ~ always will!

Part Three

Stay the Course

Bittersweet
(Life after losing the one you love)

Bittersweet.
It's my word.
Everything accomplished. Everything new.
It's bittersweet because it all comes back to you.

Bittersweet.
It's my feeling.
Every day that begins. Every day new.
It's bittersweet because it's another day without you.

Bittersweet.
It's my story.
Every moment's pleasure. Every pain anew.
It's bittersweet because it's no longer lived with you.

Chapter 14

Lessons Learned

October 16, 2013, 2:58 a.m.

Awake in the middle of the night and thinking how you are such a huge part of who I am. Moving on, but still stuck on you just the same. I miss the intimacy with you, darling—the kisses, hugs, snuggles, and making love.

I miss your touch, the feel of your hands, those back rubs you'd give me during our heart to hearts—every night except the last. You went to bed early and I stayed up. My only regret—not going to sleep with my sweetie.

No one said, "Last call."

I am nearing the end of the first year of my pilgrimage. I've had to explore unchartered territory with no choice but to endure. I've had to stand strong when I only felt weak, plug ahead when I wanted to turn back, and seek new ways to do old things. My GPS had been a well-worn road map that I referred to often, the Bible, and though it was all new to me, my guide had led others along similar paths before me. I would never be the same from the inside out, and though I could only see an end, God offered an opportunity for me to grow in His word and love. My faith had been tested. Tough love at its finest, a time to count blessings when I only felt loss.

I found I am no longer a morning person. Is it because my whole routine has been torn from me like a tornado wreaks havoc? Or is it because my life was taken from me in the morning hours? Perhaps it is because I seldom make a pot of coffee now as the smell of the coffee and the sound of it brewing scream at me that no one is here to share it with me. The newspaper no longer waits on the front porch as the crossword puzzles from last fall still anticipate my attention; I cancelled the paper months ago. Perhaps one day I will revel in the mornings again, but that time just isn't now.

Willie always told me chocolate would fix anything. That still makes me smile as I can see his face while he stood holding a bag of dark chocolates in one hand and a tall glass of milk in the other, always ready to help me make a rough day better. I don't think he ever felt like a chocolate bunny though, looking whole and complete on the outside, but hollow on the inside. I learned how that bunny feels.

I learned that I can sleep alone; I just don't sleep much. I learned I liked sharing my covers, my pillows, and my side of the bed. I learned I miss the swearing in the morning, the sound of the television at one a.m., and the blaring of the oldies station on the radio. The little things that sometimes become huge issues and in the master plan, they matter so little.

I learned I liked the feel of an unshaven face, wet curls, and a hand on my hip. I learned I can close my eyes and see the twinkle in his eyes, the grin on his face, and a tie dye T-shirt in church.

I learned I still love gardening; I just prefer to do it in the rain now. The raindrops can feel so cleansing. I still love antiques, but they are bittersweet as there is no one to share my enthusiasm. I still hate grocery shopping; I just hate it even more now.

I learned I can install window wells, refinish floors, and paint woodwork. I learned work keeps me from wasting the days I have been given. I learned I can get through the day, but only because God leads the way and provides the strength. I learned I can survive the pain of a tattoo; I am just not sure I can survive the pain of losing the one I love. That remains to be seen. Each step of my pilgrimage brings me one step closer to my Lord and Savior, and after all, isn't that my final destination?

> *But even if you should suffer for what is right, you are blessed. 1 Peter 3:14a*

October 16, 2013

I'm feeling so empty. I always thought I couldn't live without you. Now, I find I must.

Her Turn

I sat alone in the waiting room, trying to remember the last time I had seen my nurse practitioner. Willie had told me to get my physical. "How are you going to take care of people if you don't take care of yourself?" I can still see him shaking his head.

Why is it that we put off the things our loved ones want us to do until they're gone? I stared straight ahead, through floor-to-ceiling windows. Outside, dark clouds cast a gloomy glow, matching my mood.

I shifted my gaze to the decor. Chairs bordered the entire room, their seats covered with maroon, burnt orange, and olive green rectangles overlapping on an asparagus-green background. Small tables had been interjected here and there, their tops covered with magazines—*Good Housekeeping, Arthritis Today, Time.*

Time. Willie's favorite magazine. Everything brought me back to him.

A metal cane clicking against the slate tile beckoned my attention, and I looked up to see an elderly woman entering the clinic. Her disheveled gray hair surrounded a face that seemed to have lost its glow. She wore a pale blue flowered blouse buttoned askew over navy slacks, the right pant leg inadvertently tucked into a white crew sock.

Hmmm. That about sums up how I've felt all year, unable to pay attention to details.

She headed in the direction of the waiting room, and I went back to staring out the windows. The click of the cane changed as she passed from the tile to the thin beige Berber carpet, the intensity of the noise increasing as she neared me. She chose her seat.

Great. The whole waiting room empty and she has to sit right next to me.

"Good morning." I forced myself to speak.

"I suppose," she responded. "I've lost my husband of sixty-five years, so I'm not sure anymore."

"I'm sorry," I said and meant it.

"You know, it seems everything reminds me of him. I feel so lonely . . . Don't get me wrong. My kids are good. One of them is always there during the day to keep me company, but the nights . . ." She paused and I saw the tears well up in her green eyes. "The nights are so long."

I reached out and squeezed her hand. Over the past year, I had learned how important the human touch could be. "I could imagine," I said, tears threatening to fill my own eyes. "Tell me about him."

In my mind, thoughts of my own loss darted around. Memories of the one I loved. The long, lonely nights. The mornings. Oh, how I hated the mornings. But I didn't say a word. I knew she needed to talk and needed someone to listen.

Just listen.

"Deborah." The nurse stood at the doorway to the waiting room.

I squeezed the elderly woman's hand once again. "Pray for strength every day," I said. "God won't let you down. I'll pray for you, too."

"Thank you, sweetie," she said, with a hint of a smile. "Thank you."
I turned and walked away.

Sweetie. Willie always called me Sweetie. Thank you, God.

Somehow I knew with God's help, we would both be all right.

> *Do nothing out of selfish ambition or vain conceit, but
> in humility consider others better than yourselves.
> Each of you should look not only to your own interests,
> but also to the interests of others. Philippians 2:3-4*

October 18, 2013

Today, it has been a year, but my heart hurts like it was only yesterday.

No Ordinary Day

October 18 was no ordinary day.

To the rest of the world, it may have been just another day, but to me, never again would it be a day like any other. The day would always be one to remember as it marked the anniversary of Willie's passing, a painful reminder of the day my journey took an unexpected detour.

The sadness in my heart felt like enough of an illness to keep me in bed the entire day, but Rachael ensured I had plans, so I forced myself out of bed. The warm waters of the shower soothed me physically and helped wash away the tears. Nothing touched the emptiness inside. "Do the next thing," I reminded myself. "Do the next thing."

Inside the medicine cabinet, I found the candy apple red lipstick. Perhaps I had deceived myself all year, but it still seemed like a distraction from my sad eyes. After applying it, I rolled my lips together, stirring up images of Willie and his ChapStick, those soft and tender lips I missed.

Closing my eyes, I exhaled a breath from somewhere deep within.

"It'll get easier," they all said. Easier. What exactly did that mean? Nothing appeared easy today. The silence that surrounded me as I dressed differed from the turmoil that had occurred at this time last year. The silence reminded me of the love I lost. Truly, deadening, silence.

Once I finished dressing, I donned my fall jacket, the belt pulled snuggly at the waist and the scarf wrapped to hug me at the neck. I missed being held, being hugged. "Oh, how I miss you, darling," I whispered.

Tears welled up in my eyes as they had so many times through the year, so it seemed best to get out of the house. A cool gust of autumn wind touched my face as I stepped out the back door. Geese honked overhead and the dried reeds of blue fescue grasses rustled. Tumbled leaves crunched under my feet. Though most of the plants had entered dormancy, I embarked on my usual route of touring the garden beds. At one time, I enjoyed this time of year, tucking away the gardens, preparing for spring surprises. Not anymore.

The gardens seemed particularly empty today. For the most part, the garden decor had been relegated to the garden shed. The plants, including the Shasta daisies and brown-eyed Susans, had given up for the year. The lawn, void of color, lay covered with fallen leaves and turning brown. Definitely not much to see.

As I rounded the corner of the garden shed, I spied it there next to the inverted rain barrel. Blinking twice, it still appeared to be a blossom. Should I backtrack or clean my glasses? I moved in for a closer look. Hmmm. A lone yellow iris in bloom. Cool, fall weather made this time of year unfavorable for iris to come into flower. Puzzled, I furrowed my brow.

Shaking my head, I resumed my tour. More brown plants. More brown grass. More leaves that had plummeted to the ground. Several glances back to the rain barrel confirmed I had not lost my mind. The yellow iris stood tall and proud. Then I beheld another flower, this one a candy custard yellow daylily. In this part of the country, daylilies bloomed midsummer, not October. Moving nearer, I confirmed the blooming of a single yellow daylily.

Visions of yellow ribbons tied around the trunks of trees flashed in my mind. The hope of welcoming someone home tied right there in those ribbons. Yellow, the color of sunshine and optimism. Gifts from God right here before my eyes in the color honoring one's spiritual life and representing the marriage covenant.

Willie never believed in coincidences. "Everything happens for a reason, darling," he'd always tell me. These flowers were no different. God escorted me right there in the garden as He had all along.

Silently I prayed, "Oh, Lord, if you can make the flowers bloom in these conditions, surely you will help me bloom again. Thank you for always being here with me, holding me on those long, lonely nights, and for providing me strength when I felt no energy left to go on. This journey I am taking will not end today, but I know I am not alone. The conditions may not be right as far as I can see, but Lord, you've been known to do the impossible. Thank you for helping me to see that you are always with me. Amen."

The tears I wiped from my cheeks were not tears of despair, but tears of hope. My pilgrimage would continue with God my companion and the Bible my roadmap. The grief journey has no clear-cut ending. Today would mark the end of the first year, but in essence, also, a beginning.

Closing my eyes, I smiled. Not every autumn day gives you spring flowers.

October 18 was no ordinary day.

"Consider how the lilies grow. They do not labor or spin. Yet I tell you, not even Solomon in all his splendor was dressed like one of these." Luke 12:27.

In loving memory of William Young

Epilogue

The Months Before Willie's Passing

March 2012

Willie is referred to a pain clinic to manage his chronic pain. Even though his kidney and liver function tests come back normal, he is prescribed fentanyl patches and taken off hydrocodone to protect his organs.

April 2012

"Hey, Sweetie. I'm home," I called as I sat my things down on the oak table. Hearing no response, I headed to the bedroom where I could hear the *Star Trek* theme song.

"When did you get home?" Willie asked as he turned his sleepy head toward me.

"Just now," I said, walking around the bed so I could sit next to him. "Are you feeling okay?" I asked as I reached out to hug him. "You're burning up, Sweetie. You shouldn't have all those blankets on."

He yanked the covers up tighter around his neck. "I have the chills."

"Have you been like this all day?" He nodded. "Did you call the doctor?"

"He'll see me tomorrow morning," he said. The talking caused him to wheeze, and if he'd had the energy, he'd of been coughing, too.

***

Willie returns to the pain clinic. He had already been seen by his general practitioner for his fever, chills, shortness of breath, and wheezing, but is still suffering from them. I wondered if these symptoms were a result of this new medication. I recalled when Willie had been treated for pneumonia for three months only to find out it had been a reaction to a new medication. They are not concerned at the clinic.

No improvement in pain has occurred and the fentanyl dosage is increased.

May 2012

"Sweetie, you need to eat something. How about I fix you some soup with the juice?" I asked. Willie typically had no problems eating. Even after his many surgeries, he immediately asked, "When can I get something to eat?"

"I can't. I feel like I'm gonna throw up." He sat up on the edge of the bed. "Where's my cane?" he asked. Puzzled, I went to get the cane that hung on the stair railing by the back door. Though the cane proved a necessity for balance on long walks, he normally maneuvered indoors easily.

I changed the damp bed linens while he went to the bathroom. Why did he feel so bad and why didn't the medication help?

As I tucked him back into bed, I listened to his labored breathing. The bathroom adjoined the bedroom and he should not have been panting.

I shut the light off and prayed. "God, give me some help here."

***

At the pain clinic, Willie reports no improvement in function. Walking has become more difficult and his balance is off. We discuss his loss of appetite and the nausea. He is losing weight. Sleeping consumes most of his days. He is winded as he speaks, wheezing and coughing between short phrases. The fentanyl dosage is decreased.

June 2012

Willie and I return to the pain clinic. He continues to suffer from fever, chills, coughing, and wheezing. The shortness of breath is evident as he walks into the clinic and back to the exam room. His balance continues to worsen and he relies more on the cane. No change is made in the fentanyl medication.

July 2012

I watched Willie out the kitchen window while I tested the water temperature with my fingertips. Dressed in a threadbare black T-shirt and cut-off blue jeans, he exited the service door of the garage carrying a black vinyl-covered card table.

I smiled as I glanced away to plug the sink. He sure enjoyed these sunshiny days so he could refinish old wooden shipping crates, and I celebrated that he felt well enough to do so. The antique show wasn't until September, but he always prepared months in advance.

As I looked back up, I saw Willie drop the card table, one leg of it extended, as he stumbled backwards, nearly falling into the porch post on the beehive yellow playhouse. He reached for it and once he steadied himself, he shook his head, pulled off his cap, and ran his fingers through his hair.

Once the cap had been replaced on his head, he stepped forward, grabbed the card table and attempted to pull out another leg, but his movements were ataxic (a lack of muscle coordination) and he struggled.

"Bud, was your dad okay this morning?" I hollered as I continued to watch Willie fight to do something he had done numerous times.

"What?" I could hear the annoyance in his voice as he turned the volume down on the television.

"When you and your dad went up north this morning, was he . . . Never mind," I said as I shut off the water and grabbed a dish towel to dry my hands. "Come and help me get your dad off the ground."

Bud followed me out the back door and across a patch of green lawn to the area by the little cedar bridge that led to the playhouse. While I knelt down by Willie, Bud moved the card table.

I slid my left arm under Willie's shoulders and picked his upper body off the ground. "Are you alright, Sweetie?"

"I don't know what's the matter with me," he said, his voice quavering, his eyes puzzled, fearful.

"Maybe you just need to lie down for a little bit," I said. "Bud, help me get your dad into the house."

Bud and I helped Willie up and walked him to the house. He needed both of us to steady him. Once inside the house, we provided support while he ascended three steps, went through the kitchen, down the hallway, and finally to the bedroom, where he sat on the edge of the bed and hung his head. I knelt down to slip his shoes off.

"I'm sorry, Sweetie," he said.

As I stood, I placed my hand on his left shoulder. "C'mon. Just lie down, Sweetie. There's nothing to be sorry about. Get some rest and I'll come back and check on you." I pulled the damask comforter up over his shoulder and kissed his cheek.

"I'm sorry, Sweetie. I don't know what's wrong with me."

He looked dazed.

I sat sideways on the edge of the bed, steadying myself with one barefoot on the beige carpet. "Shhh. It's alright, darling," I said while I rubbed his back. "Just get some rest. Shhh."

Before long, I heard the familiar snore. I slid off the edge of the bed, noting the red glowing numbers on the clock read nearly noon. As I quietly closed the door, I prayed. "Lord, is he having another stroke? Is something else wrong? Should I force him to go the emergency room even though he sees the doctor this week? I just don't know."

Worried, I checked on Willie several times throughout the afternoon and evening. He barely stirred when I crawled into bed that night or out of bed in the morning. Twenty-four hours later, he continued to sleep. He didn't even get up to go to the bathroom. I stood in the doorway, head leaning into the door frame and my arms crossed over my chest, watching him.

As Bud came down the stairs, he said, "What's wrong, Ma?"

"Just worried about your dad."

"He's just tired, Ma. Don't worry." He gave me a little hug and I knew he worried, too.

***

The seven o'clock hour approached and Willie still slept.

"Hey, Ma. Do you think Dad is getting up for wrestling?" Bud asked. The two of them had watched *Monday Night Wrestling* since Bud had been two years old. They never missed a week.

I laid the newspaper aside and stood up from my perch on the black leather sofa. "I'll go ask him. He's been sleeping an awfully long time," I said.

Willie still lay on his right side on the bed, his arm hanging over the edge. I nudged his shoulder gently as I called out to him. "Sweetie . . . Sweetie." I put more force behind my nudges.

159

He half-opened his eyes. "What?" he mumbled.

"I just wondered if you were going to watch wrestling with your son tonight."

Willie opened his eyes wide and sat up abruptly.

"What the hell happened to Sunday?" he demanded.

August 2012

"His balance hasn't been good and he's even fallen," I said. "And his memory is worse. I've been worried he had another stroke. And it seems all he does now is sleep."

"I'm just so damn tired," Willie said.

"Mm, hmm. What about the pain?" the healthcare provider asked. "Are the patches helping?"

"Can't I try something different?" Willie said, rubbing the side of his head as he spoke. "I don't like this patch. I felt better taking the pain pills."

"What don't you like about the patch?" the healthcare provider asked.

"I don't know." Willie shook his head. "It just makes me feel funny."

"What do you mean?"

"I don't know. I just don't feel like myself."

"I can't really give you anything else then," the healthcare provider said as she typed notes into her computer. I imagined it as if she had a red ink pad and a rubber stamp. In big, bold letters it would read: REQUEST DENIED.

***

On a sunny afternoon, Willie and I boarded the SS Badger ferry at Manitowoc, Wisconsin, and headed across Lake Michigan to Ludington, Michigan. A dream come true for him, he smiled as he stretched out his sandaled feet on a royal blue lounge chair. He reminded me of a delighted child and I winked at him from my place by the railing. He tilted his head twice to the left, scooted over on the chair, and patted the spot next to him. How could I resist?

We stayed in Ludington our first two nights in Michigan. We held hands as we walked on the beach, visited local shops, and went down to the lighthouse pier to welcome the ferry as it sailed in.

When we left Ludington, we headed north on US-31. Willie pulled into the parking lot of the Empire Bluffs and turned the volume down on the radio.

"What are we doing here?" I asked.

"I thought you wanted to get a different view of Lake Michigan," he answered.

I sat up and put my tennis shoes on. "Thanks, Sweetie."

Once we exited the butane blue van, we walked over to the brown national park sign and read it. "Sweetie, we don't have to do this. It's a mile and a half to the top and it looks like there are lots of ups and downs," I said.

"Let's go," he said, prodding me along with his wooden cane.

"Are you sure?" I asked, pleading with my eyes. Again with the cane.

The hike up the bluffs resembled maneuvering an obstacle course as we scaled inclines, irregular steps built from railroad ties and pea-sized gravel, and some narrow passageways. The view from the top was heavenly, but I could tell Willie had gone through hell.

***

An inn not far from there provided us with lodging that night. Willie moaned several times through the night and I was sure the day's adventures had increased his pain. Why couldn't the doctors see this method of pain control didn't work for him? His body ached; my heart ached.

***

"Good morning, Sweetie," Willie said as he came through the door, his cane in one hand and a tract in the other. "Ha, ha. Guess what I got?" Grinning, he flipped it around so I could see. Written in bold black Old English letters, it read, "Antiques."

I took it from him. "Oh good. Most of these look like they are just off the highway."

After breakfast, we pulled the flyer out again and mapped our course. Willie opted to drive. He seemed to tolerate that best in the mornings. At some point in the afternoon, I would take over.

"Leland. That's funny. I didn't know there was a Leland in any other state," I said. Willie knew my grandparents had lived in Leland, Illinois, at one time.

"You never know, dear. Now, watch the street signs." He sounded irritated.

Even though Leland appeared to be a small community, people filled the sidewalks and vacant parking spots were in short supply. I felt like we were in Door County, Wisconsin, in the summertime.

The third pass through town, I spotted a sign. "That's what all the fuss is about, Sweetie. Sidewalk Sales."

He slammed on the brakes and glared at me. "Do you think this is funny?"

"What are you talking about?"

"That's it." He put the van in reverse, carelessly backed up, and made a spot to park along the side of the road. After forcefully shifting into park, he pulled out the keys, banged the door shut, and started walking away, leaving me sitting there wondering what just happened. No "Oh well, guess we'll have an adventure." Just pure agitation.

Unsure when—and if—he intended to return, I got out of the van myself and began exploring the area. I looked, but did not see. Concentrating was challenging. Had Dr. Jekyll transformed my mild-mannered husband into Mr. Hyde?

Much time had passed when I saw Willie hobbling toward me. His cane pounding into the blacktop told me his demeanor remained edgy, not apologetic. "What the hell do you think you're doing walking around in a strange city with all these people around?" He shook his cane in the air. "Anything could have happened to you." He turned to walk away. I followed.

He led me to the beach and we walked. No holding hands. No conversation. Just walking. Physically, I could see him ten steps ahead of me, but inside, I had no idea where he was.

Back in the van, Willie, now seated on the passenger side, peered out the window. "I don't know what's wrong with me," he said. "Let's just get out of here."

We went as far as Manistee, where we checked into the Riverside, a quaint little motel on the marina.

"It's only 4:30, darling. That'll give us plenty of time to find a place for supper," I said as we took the luggage out of the van.

"Do you mind if I lay down for a little bit, Sweetie?"

"No, that's okay. We can go get something to eat when you get up," I said.

He gave me a quick kiss on the cheek before lying down on top of the bed linens, fully dressed right down to his shoes. I think he fell asleep immediately.

By 6:30, I had all but given up on going out to supper. I went out to the van and got the Ziploc baggie of grape tomatoes we had brought with us from home and went out the sliding glass doors to sit on the patio. As I sat in the lounge chair, I eyed the grill sitting next door. The smell of charcoal filled the air. I popped another grape tomato into my mouth.

Beyond the patio, a flight of steps led down to the water. After checking on Willie and writing him a note, I took the twenty-some steps down to the riverwalk. The four-slat wooden railing that guarded either side of the wooden planked walkway reminded me of the pasture fencing at the farm.

The evening air felt good and the still waters contributed to the calmness. As I walked toward Lake Michigan, I found so many things I wanted to point out to Willie, but instead, I reviewed the day's events. What was going on with him? Why was he so edgy? And who goes on vacation and spends their time sleeping in a motel room bed?

I missed him. Something was not right.

***

"Willie. Willie, did you want to take a shower before we check out?" I asked, nudging his shoulder. It seemed all I did lately as Willie slept the days away.

"What time is it?" he asked, rolling over in bed.

"It's 10:30 and checkout is at 11:00." I sat down on the bed next to him.

"Why didn't you wake me up for supper?"

"You seemed awfully tired." I attempted a smile. Truth be told, I had no idea what mood he'd be in if I had woke him.

"Did you eat something then?" He reached out and rubbed my knee.

"Grape tomatoes."

"Oh, Sweetie. I'm sorry." He gave me a hug before heading to the shower.

I stayed on the bed and listened to the water run and Willie curse and moan. Was the pain out of control or was he coming down with something? What would this day bring?

***

"Ready for breakfast?" Willie said as he finished dressing. "Silly

164

question. You are probably starving since I deserted you for supper. C'mon. Let's go."

Willie sat behind the steering wheel, leaning forward to insert the key in the ignition. He sat back and attempted to take in a deep breath. "You mind driving?" He patted at his chest. "Chest is feeling a little tight this morning. You know, that stuff I always get."

I drove to breakfast. After the waitress poured our coffee, I watched Willie add his two sugar packets. It took effort to pick up the spoon and stir. His breathes, short and shallow, barely moved his chest. He looked out the window as he sipped, and though just across the table, I felt him miles away. Tears stung my eyes.

He coughed and slapped at his chest again. "When did you say our tickets back were?"

I resisted the urge to say I've told you that several times already. After sipping my coffee and setting down my cup, I answered. "They are open-ended, Sweetie. We just need to call the day we want to head home."

I stared out the window where bright blue skies shone, but my mind focused on Willie's foggy memory. Since his stroke, he had difficulty retrieving the right words. But this was more than that.

"Did you hear me, Sweetie?" Willie said as he reached out and gently touched my arm. I raised my eyebrows as I looked at him. "I thought we could head home tonight," he repeated.

For over ten years, he talked about this trip, and now he wanted to go home early.

September 2012

Seven rings. Was he sleeping again? Two more rings and the answering machine would pick up.

"Hello."

Did I detect agitation in his voice again? I took a deep breath. "Hey, Sweetie. I've just got a couple minutes, but I was wondering how it went at the doctor's this morning," I said.

"Those son of a b----. They treat me like I'm a drug dealer or something. They don't listen. They never listen," he said. The condescending remarks I heard from other healthcare providers about people who needed pain medications played in my head. Drug abusers. Drug users. Frequent flyers. They're only after the drugs.

"I'm sorry, Sweetie. I wish I could have gone with you."

Couldn't those people see this man hurt? This man, my husband, who once enjoyed playing football in the backyard with his son until the pain prevented it. This man who once wrestled with his children in the living room until I demanded they stop before something broke. This man who once walked the neighborhood holding my hand until the pain limited us to around the block, then the block, and finally, to no walks at all.

This man. My husband. Father to my children. A man in pain— daily.

"I told them to schedule you when I could bring you," I continued.

"I'm telling you. They don't listen. I told them where to stick it this morning and left," he said.

"Darling, you didn't." My shoulders dropped. My head hurt. When did he get such a short fuse?

"Yes, I did." He paused and I could hear his labored breaths. "Don't worry, Sweetie. I went back about 11:30. What else am I gonna do?"

"Did they take you off the patch?"

"They increased it," he said.

"What?" My turn to be disgruntled.

"Get back to work. I'm going to go work on some things for the show. I'll see you when you get home."

A click ended the conversation and I sat staring at the receiver as though it would resolve all my issues.

***

I reached out for him when I woke up, but he no longer lay next to me. After donning my pink plaid robe and sliding my feet into my slippers, I headed to the kitchen where I thought I'd find him sitting at the table, his hair wild on his head and a cup of coffee in his hand. I discovered the kitchen empty, but the back door stood open and I could see Willie and Bud hard at work.

"Good morning, guys. This is quite the surprise,"" I said over the squeak of the screen door.

"Show's coming up in a few weeks. Gotta get things done," Willie said. "Besides, I feel pretty good today. He held his varnish-filled paint brush aside to give me a kiss.

Bud groaned. "Yea. Gotta get things done."

"What's wrong kiddo? I thought you liked to do the shows," I asked.

"I do. I just don't like getting up so freaking early," he answered. I laughed as I headed back indoors for my own cup of coffee.

As I sipped coffee from a white ceramic mug, I watched father and son, working side-by-side, talking and laughing. They had their own system, each sitting at a card table to varnish, and when completed, transferring their wares to a series of tables aligned in the September sunshine for drying.

Willie had been purchasing inventory for his retirement for at least twenty years, so they had plenty to do. I smiled and could hear him in my mind saying, "It's money in the bank, Sweetie," and I could almost feel the kiss that always followed. But watching father and son, I knew this amounted to so much more than money in the bank.

I smiled, happy that Willie had been able to take early retirement last October and he could spend this time with his son. Having lost my dad when I hadn't been much older than Bud, I knew what this time meant.

Willie taught Bud to sand furniture when he was still a toddler, and the antique shows had become their thing. Quality time together, preparing for it together and then setting up and selling for a day. The conversations that must take place on the two-hour ride down and the ride back. I grinned again. While they bonded the day of the show, I would have the day to myself. I treasured the thought. Those days did not happen often.

***

What the heck? As I pulled up to the driveway after working all day, I could see the doors and the back hatch of the van open. Willie and Bud should have had the van loaded for the show. They needed to leave in the wee hours of the morning.

I parked the truck and did not see anyone around as I got out. Inside, the keys clanked as I tossed them on the kitchen table. "Hello," I called out as I headed toward the bedroom. "Willie?" As I flipped the light on, Bud's footsteps could be heard coming down the stairs.

"What's going on, Bud? How come you guys aren't loaded up?"

"Dad said he needed to lie down for a little bit," Bud answered.

Willie sat up on the edge of the bed. "I'm not feeling good at all. I don't think I'll be able to do the show tomorrow." He rubbed the pale skin at his temples and shook his head. "I've never felt this bad."

I dropped my shoulders and sighed. "Lie down, honey. Bud and I will load the van and we'll see how you feel in the morning." I clicked the light off. "Don't expect your perfection though," I called out as I walked away.

The task took longer with just Bud and me. Willie could fill every square inch of the van when he did a show. He had an eye for how things would fit together to make the best use of the space. All his wares would sit in the backyard like giant puzzle pieces, and he instructed Bud and me how to stack them for the space available.

"What if Dad doesn't feel better in the morning?" Bud asked as he handed me another stack of shipping crates.

"He never misses a show, Bud. He lives for these shows. You know he'll get up and go."

***

I suddenly pushed myself up on my elbow and reached over Willie to shut the blaring fifties music off. 3:00 a.m. Normally, when he and Bud did a show, Willie would quietly dress and leave before I even realized it.

"Willie . . . Willie . . . Hey, Sweetie, are you and Bud going to do the show?" I asked in a whisper.

"I can't, dear. I just can't." He rolled over. "All that work for nothing."

I flung the blankets aside, sat up, and started getting dressed. "Don't worry. I'll go with Bud," I said.

"You don't have to do that, Sweetie."

"I know, but you invested a lot of time and I didn't have any specific plans. It will be a good day for Bud and me to bond. At least he'll know what he's doing." I laughed, more to ease Willie's worries than anything.

In the kitchen, Bud poured coffee into to-go cups. As I came into the room, he switched out Willie's chartreuse green one for my royal blue one. "He's really not going?" I shook my head. "Something is really wrong, Ma. Dad loves doing the shows."

"I know. He's just not having a good weekend. Let's go." As I tried to reassure him, my own worrisome thoughts nagged me. We headed for the backdoor. "Just know, I am not wearing that goofy hat."

"It's our trademark, Ma. Dad would wear it." He held up the Green Bay Packers visors with the green and gold fake fur hair. "You gotta wear it."

"I'm not your dad," I said as we got into the van.

His eyes betrayed him, letting me know he had looked forward to this day with his dad. And I knew Willie had felt the same, but this morning, Willie's health kept him in bed, too sick and too weak, to even see us off.

I took the visor from Bud.

October 5, 2012

Willie returns to the pain clinic where blood is drawn for laboratory tests to check the fentanyl levels. The sample is shipped to another state for testing.

October 17, 2012

I punched out right at five o'clock, but I didn't find him waiting for me in the parking lot, so I put my things down on the bench and sat where I had a view of the street. Silence, a rare gift, surrounded me and I relished it.

Shortly, I saw our van speeding down the street, barely slowing enough to make the left turn into the parking lot. I smiled as I gathered my belongings. Time management had not been a virtue Willie carried into retirement.

As I climbed into the passenger side, he looked at me quite seriously. "I gotta tell ya, dear. Don't get use to this." he said.

I frowned as I buckled my seat belt. Picking me up from work was an exception to the rule, but happened today due to his truck being in the garage and his need to see his general practitioner for his continued shortness of breath, wheezing, and cough.

Sensing my disappointment, he reached out and shook my leg. Tilting his head so his face was aligned with mine and raising his eyebrows, he said, "Or do you want to?"

I smiled at him. Of course, I wanted to get used to being picked up and dropped off at the door.

Little did I realize it would be the last time he ever picked me up and the last day we would spend together.

The Months After Willie's Passing

The sound of the back door latching was barely audible over the geese honking overhead as they headed south for the winter. Another season of change had arrived.

I pushed the screen door shut and glanced at my gold watch with the sparkling stones surrounding its white face. Months had passed before I dared slip it on my wrist again. Time had stopped when Willie died and I felt it would never start again.

Seven o'clock. Laundry nearly done. Tootsie cared for. My bed made.

I wrapped the beige giraffe-print scarf gently around my neck before unlatching the garden gate. At some point, I enjoyed the morning walks again, the crunch of brown leaves beneath my feet. I breathed in the crisp autumn air and brushed my hair back from my face where the breeze had blown it.

The brightly colored leaves waved from lofty branches as I walked by. Soon, they too would fall, assembling on the concrete sidewalk, forming a carpeted layer for me to tread upon. The trees would survive, just as I had.

"Three years, Sweetie, and somehow I have survived," I whispered to the wind. Three years. I strolled on, slowing my steps to reflect on my journey.

Occasional tears fill my eyes. I suppose they always will. A gentle reminder that I had loved, blessed with the joy of having shared life with Willie. More often I smile—or laugh—as I recall the time God loaned him to me.

I learned new things—basket weaving, making toothbrush rag rugs—and I've begun perfecting old ones—crocheting, photography, writing. Time is valued—and short—so I relish it, not always doing something; sometimes just enjoying the moment. Being alone or with others. Listening to music, nature, or nothing at all.

I no longer have to tell myself to do the next thing; I just do it. My routine has changed, but I have one. I enjoy life again.

"God has granted me opportunities to help others, Sweetie. Others who have lost loved ones. I never understood before, but I do now. I'll always miss you, but I can—and have—survived."

Information for Healthcare Providers & Patient Advocates

Here are the things I wish I had known. I pray they help anyone who is dealing with pain, loves someone who suffers with pain, or treats someone who is a chronic pain sufferer, especially if they are using fentanyl.

What is fentanyl?

First developed in 1959, fentanyl is a synthetic opioid, a narcotic that is prescribed for chronic pain. A Duragesic patch contains the fentanyl in a gel form. It is released gradually into the patient's skin.

Precautions when using fentanyl

1. As with all medications, do not take other prescription or over-the-counter medications, including supplements, without discussing them with your doctor, or better yet, your pharmacist. Certain substances will increase the effects of central nervous system depressants. These include, but are not limited to:
- Alcohol
- Antihistamines often used for allergies or colds
- Sedatives
- Tranquilizers or other sleeping medications
- Other pain medications
- Seizure medications
- Barbiturates
- Muscle relaxants
- Anesthetics

I also suggest checking other medications that you or your loved one are taking that have similar side effects such as "respiratory depression." In addition to the fentanyl, my husband had two other medications with that same side effect.

2. Heat speeds the absorption of fentanyl into the body, therefore increasing the serious side effects. Consider all sources of heat, not just a heating pad. Do not use or do any of the following:

- Heating pad
- Electric blanket
- Heat lamp
- Sauna
- Heated water bed
- Long, hot shower or bath
- Sunbathing
- Running a fever

How can overdoses occur?

In addition to drug interactions and heat, an overdose can result if fentanyl is prescribed to someone for acute pain, including post-surgical or short-term, or to someone who is not opiate-tolerant. It's also possible for a defective Duragesic patch to allow medication to be released rapidly. The medication is to be released over seventy-two hours, not rapidly.

How are fentanyl levels monitored?

Due to the risk of toxicity, fentanyl levels should be monitored. This can be done with a simple blood test. I encourage you to find out where the lab work is being done. The clinic my husband utilized had their lab work done out-of-state, delaying the time it took to get results.

What are the signs and symptoms of fentanyl toxicity?

- Inability to think, walk, or talk normally*
- Feeling faint, dizzy, confused, or agitated*
- Alterations in mood*

* Cite specific incidents and ask the healthcare provider to repeat them back to you. Make sure they are listening. For example, my husband's medical record did note he had balance issues. What does that mean? Is he frequently falling down? Afraid to walk without furniture walking? Does he stumble on occasion? Is his balance fine when he stands still? Progress or decline is impossible to denote if there is no baseline. Ask questions and listen to the answers.

- Respiratory depression: Labored, shallow or stopped breathing
- Extreme sleepiness, severe enough to interfere with your activities for more than a few days. Is the person telling you they are having a hard time getting out of bed? Dig deeper. How much sleep do they usually get? There's that baseline again. How long are they sleeping now? Is it interfering with their activity?
- Clammy, cold skin
- Seizures
- Low blood pressure
- Loss of consciousness
- Small pupils
- Compromised heart beat

What to do if you suspect toxicity?

Call 911 immediately. Make sure the first responders know the victim is using the fentanyl patch. Emergency medications and opiate antagonists like NARCAN and naloxone can be used to counteract the effects of a fentanyl overdose.

Be informed. Be persistent. Listen. This isn't about getting the paperwork done or going through the motions. It is about quality of life for living beings who are seeking to live pain-free.

Resources

For additional information, see these websites, which were current at the time of this publishing:

http://harborvillageflorida.com/glossary/drugs/fentanyl/overdose-and-toxicity-of-fentanyl/

http://www.legaltube.com/breaking-news-hot-list/fentanyl/drug-warning-signs-and-symptoms-of-fentanyl-toxicity.aspx

http://www.mayoclinic.org/drugs-supplements/fentanyl-transdermal-route/precautions/drg-20068152

http://novusdetox.com/fentanyl-patch.php

© 2005 WebMD, Inc. All rights reserved.
http://www.webmd.com/pain-management/news/20050715/deaths-seen-with-fentanyl-narcotic-pain-patch

Dealing with Grief

GriefShare—You do not have to grieve alone. To find a group near you or learn more about GriefShare, visit the website @ http://www.griefshare.org/ OR email info@griefshare.org OR call 800-395-5755.

About the Author

Deborah Young, the middle of five children, resides in Green Bay, Wisconsin. Born in Illinois en route to the hospital, she later moved to Wisconsin, where she became an avid Green Bay Packers fan. As a young girl, she showed an interest in reading and writing, and carried that love with her wherever she went. Her publishing credits include pieces in the *Green Bay Press-Gazette*, the *Beloit Daily News*, *The Voice*, *PT Connections*, *The Chimes* newsletter of St. Mary's Hospital Medical Center, and *Green Prints*. Her other hobbies include crocheting, rug making, going to flea markets, and vegetable and flower gardening.

Deborah is a member of Our Saviour Lutheran Church in Green Bay, where she is active in the Lutheran Women's Missionary League, Chix with Stix, and Bible Studies. She is also a founding member of their Christian Writers Group. Deborah worked in healthcare for most of her adult life. She currently works as a physical therapist assistant, where she strives to empower others. Deborah is mother to two daughters, a son, and a tuxedo cat named Tootsie.

Made in the USA
Lexington, KY
02 June 2016